Social Statistics in Ireland

By the same author

Irish Economic Statistics

(with G.J. Bourke) *Interpretation and Uses of Medical Statistics*

SOCIAL STATISTICS IN IRELAND

A Guide to their Sources and Uses

JAMES McGILVRAY

INSTITUTE OF PUBLIC ADMINISTRATION
DUBLIN

© James McGilvray 1977
Published by
Institute of Public Administration
59 Lansdowne Road
Dublin 4   Ireland

ISBN O 902173 74 X

Set in 11 on 12 point Press Roman

Printed in Ireland by Cahill (1976) Ltd., East Wall Road, Dublin 3.

CONTENTS

Preface   ix
1   Basic Demographic Statistics   1
2   Vital Statistics   17
3   Health   36
4   Housing   57
5   Education   72
6   Social Security   81
7   Incomes, Expenditure and the Standard
     of Living   98
8   Other Social Statistics   128
9   Some Statistical Concepts   139
10   Survey Methods in Social Research   168
     Index   200

ABBREVIATIONS AND GLOSSARY

CPI	Consumer Price Index
CSO	Central Statistics Office
DSW	Department of Social Welfare
ESB	Electricity Supply Board
ESRI	The Economic and Social Research Institute
FES	*Family Expenditure Survey*
GNP	Gross National Product
HBI	Household Budget Inquiry
HEA	The Higher Education Authority
HMSO	Her Majesty's Stationery Office
ISB	*Irish Statistical Bulletin*
JNMR	*Joint National Media Research Survey*
NES	*New Earnings Survey*
OECD	Organisation for Economic Cooperation and Development
RTE	Radio Telefís Éireann
SMR	Standardised Mortality Ratio
TD	Teachta Dala (Member of the Dáil)
WHO	World Health Organisation

Bord Fáilte	The Irish Tourist Board
Bord na Móna	Irish Peat Development Authority
An Foras Forbartha	The National Institute for Physical Planning and Construction Research
An Foras Talúntais	The Agricultural Institute
Garda Síochána	Irish Police Force
Roinn na Gaeltachta	Department of the Gaeltacht

PREFACE

The modest success of *Irish Economic Statistics* suggested that a similar book on Irish social statistics might also serve a useful purpose. This volume is therefore intended as a complement to the earlier publication, and is designed to be a basic reference source and guide to published social statistics in Ireland.

A borderline between economic statistics and social statistics cannot be precisely defined, since economics is itself concerned with a particular dimension of the social system. There is therefore some overlap between the content of the two volumes, particularly with respect to population and vital statistics (chapters 1-2 of the present volume), and incomes, expenditure and the standard of living (chapter 7 in the present volume). However, there are differences in emphasis in the treatment of these subjects.

Most chapters of this book contain a brief discussion of United Kingdom and international sources of social statistics. In addition, chapter 9 provides a simple, though necessarily selective, introduction to certain statistical methods commonly employed in analysing social statistics, and chapter 10 summarises the basic concepts of sample survey methods.

Social statistics serve a wide variety of purposes. They provide valuable information about many important facets of society. The availability of such quantitative information provides impetus to the development of social policies, and influences the direction and scope of social policy. These statistics provide the essential raw material for analyses of the structure and dynamics of a social system. Economics is probably the most developed of the social sciences in the use of statistics for constructing behavioural models of social systems, but other social sciences are now making increasing use of mathematical and statistical techniques for the formulation and testing of hypotheses. Science progresses by means of the formulation and testing of hypotheses, and by the replacement of old hypotheses and theories by new ones, a progression in which statistical information, whether in the form of repeated laboratory experiments, or regular observations of social behaviour, is an indispensable element.

Even for the simplest types of description and analysis, the present provision of social statistics in Ireland is inadequate. Moreover, the statistics which are available are often not readily accessible, are badly presented, and contain little or no analytical content. (Perhaps ironically, one of the worst-served areas in terms of the supply of statistical information is education.) Compared with the quantity and quality of published economic statistics, social statistics are very poor.

This neglect is reflected in the contents of the *Irish Statistical Bulletin*, which contains barely any social statistics. The structure and content of this quarterly publication have remained substantially the same since World War II, and are badly in need of revision. The annual *Statistical Abstract* is a better reference for social statistics, but its content is usually three or four years out-of-date, and is necessarily very selective. There is therefore no regular publication which can be referred to for up-to-date information on the main series of social statistics. Simply to discover *what* social statistics are available is a formidable task for the neophyte, for whom, it is hoped, this book will prove helpful.

A number of people have helped make this book better than it would otherwise have been, though they are not responsible for its remaining failings. Helpful comments and suggestions were made by Brendan Walsh, John O'Gorman, W.J. Hyland, R. Hearne, Seamus O Cinneide, Colm McCarthy, Tony Brown, Shaun Trant, P.A.R. Hillyard, John Meagher and Des Byrne (Irish Marketing Surveys Limited), Sue Scott, and various anonymous readers in the Central Statistics Office. My wife kindly compiled the index, and Mrs Sheelagh Blackhall patiently typed and retyped the several versions of manuscript.

November 1976 James McGilvray

X

CHAPTER 1

BASIC DEMOGRAPHIC STATISTICS

DEMOGRAPHY is concerned with the study of human populations; in particular, with changes in populations. The level and composition of a population change continuously, but exact measures of the population are available only at specific moments, notably at the time of a *census*. Measures of change in population will be discussed in chapter 2. This chapter describes statistics relating to the population at particular points in time and various applications of these data.

1.1. THE CENSUS OF POPULATION

The most important source of information about the population of Ireland is the periodic census of population. The census is essentially a head count of the number of persons resident in Ireland at a specific date, but it contains in addition a considerable volume of information ranging from the age and sex composition of the population to its geographic distribution, marital status and occupational structure. The census can therefore be regarded as a social-economic profile of the population at a particular moment.

The first official census in Ireland was taken in 1841. It was repeated at ten-year intervals up to 1911, and subsequently in 1926, 1936, 1946, and at five-year intervals from that date. It is now established practice to conduct a census at intervals of five years.[1]

1. However the 1976 census was cancelled as an economy measure.

1

A certain amount of basic information is collected and published in each census: for example, the total size of population, its age and sex composition, and its geographic distribution. Certain other information may be collected from time to time, or once only. For example, the 1946, 1961 and 1971 censuses included a special section on fertility, and the 1966 census contained a special section on education. Further data on education were collected in the 1971 census.

The actual census data are collected by means of questionnaires which are distributed to each household some time prior to the census date, and the completed forms are later collected by temporary field personnel. (Completion of the census form is compulsory.) The agency responsible for collecting, processing and publishing the data is the Central Statistics Office (CSO). It is important to note that the information required on the census form relates only to persons actually resident in the household on the night of the official census date. Persons who are normally resident in the household but who were absent on the night in question are not (or should not be) included. If they are elsewhere in the country, they will be included on some other census form; if outside the boundaries of the state, they will not be included at all. Conversely, persons who are normally resident abroad but who happen to be in Ireland on the official census date will be counted as part of the population of Ireland.

> The population recorded . . . represents all persons present within [the State's] boundaries on the night of [17 April 1966], together with all persons who arrived (in the State) on the morning of [Monday, 18 April 1966], not having been enumerated elsewhere; persons aboard ships or boats in port, etc., are included with the population. . . .

Thus 'the population' is an empirical or *de facto* concept, and the population of Ireland on 17 April 1966 differs from the population on 16 April, or any other date in the year. The census is usually taken at a time of year when movements due to holidays and to other reasons are reckoned to be low.

The results of the census are published in volumes which

appear at intervals over the three or four years following the census date. Given the large volume of data which have to be processed, such a time-lag is inevitable, though the use of electronic computers for data processing and tabulation will help shorten these delays. A brief preliminary report is published soon after the census data have been collected — usually in August or September, since the census itself is normally taken in early April. Each of the subsequent census reports deals with a particular aspect of the population: age and sex composition, marital status, occupations, industries, geographic distribution, and so on. Some of these will be discussed briefly in a later section.

Apart from the census reports, summary census data are also published in the annual *Statistical Abstract,* and analyses of census data are occasionally published in the quarterly *Irish Statistical Bulletin (ISB).* Results of the 1971 census were also reported in a series of *preliminary bulletins* (see section 1.3).

1.2. USES OF CENSUS DATA

The census provides a detailed profile of the population at a particular moment. Several different, though overlapping, uses of census material can be distinguished.

First, current census data are used to portray or analyse prevalent social and economic characteristics, for example in housing, education, size of family, urban/rural occupational patterns, and so on. Analyses of this kind are usually related, directly or indirectly, to particular social or economic problems and policies. For instance, census data on housing may be used in a study of housing needs, and data on size of family for estimating the type of housing which may be required. Again, the geographical distribution of the population and its occupational structure have a bearing on regional industrial development policies. The proportion of the population who live in urban areas is often used as a rough comparative index of a country's level of development or of its level of industrialisation. It is hardly necessary to elaborate the importance of the census for these kinds of studies, and indeed the form of presentation of census data is influenced by considerations of how the material might subsequently be used. Thus many of the tables in census reports are designed in a form appropriate to the kinds of applications referred to above.

'Structural analysis' of the population at a given moment can be extended to comparative studies of changes in the structure of population over time. For example, how has the geographical distribution, or age structure, or occupational pattern of the Irish population changed in the last century? In fact very few demographic studies fail to include comparative data designed to show how a given feature of the population has changed (or remained stable) over a period of time. As a simple illustration, table 1.1. records the age structure of the female population of Ireland in 1901, 1936 and 1966. Note that the *percentage* of females in each group at each census date is also recorded; percentage data are often more illuminating than actual numbers when used for comparison. Table 1.1. is an example of a *frequency distribution* (there are three frequency distributions, one for each census year) which is commonly used in presenting statistical data.[2] Similar tables could be prepared to show, for example, how the populations of different counties had changed, absolutely and relatively, or how the occupational pattern of the working population had changed. In each case, we are classifying the population — or part of the population — in a certain way at one moment, then classifying earlier, or later, census data in exactly the same way, and comparing these

Table 1.1   **Age distribution of females in Ireland in 1901, 1936 and 1966**

Age	1901		1936		1966	
	'000	%	'000	%	'000	%
0 - 14	478.8	27.7	404.0	27.9	441.0	30.7
15 - 29	464.5	28.8	353.5	24.4	290.9	20.3
30 - 44	275.4	17.1	264.0	18.2	233.0	16.2
45 - 64	289.4	18.0	280.7	19.4	297.0	20.7
65 and over	103.4	6.4	145.8	10.1	173.1	12.1
	1611.8	100.0	1448.0	100.0	1435.0	100.0

Source: Censuses of Population 1901, 1936, 1966.

2. For a discussion of frequency distributions and other statistical concepts, see chapter 9.

distributions. It is important to look out for changes in definition or methods of classification of census data, which may invalidate comparisons over time unless the classification of census data for different years can be standardised. For example, city or town boundaries may be changed between censuses.

The main purpose of comparing census data for different years (intertemporal comparisons) is to identify any *trend* in the characteristic being studied. For example, we can classify families in the 1961 census according to the number of children per family. The distribution of families by number of children in 1961 is itself of interest, but it might also be revealing to compare this with similar distributions for, say, 1911 and 1861. From these and supplementary data and analyses, we may infer something about trends in fertility. A study of this kind would be extemely complex, utilising a considerable amount of census and other data (if available); we would also need to know something about the age distribution of the population at each date, the ages at which people married, the geographic distribution of the population, and various other data considered relevant to such an analysis. The main point, however, is that analyses of this kind are often more important for what they reveal about historical trends than for what they show about the population at a particular time. The study of ways in which particular variables such as population, or national income, or the number of registered motor vehicles change over time involves the statistical technique of *time series analysis*. This technique is explained in chapter 9, but the principal purpose of time series analysis is to identify historical trends, if any, in the particular variable or attribute being studied. More hazardously, attempts may be made to project such trends into the future. One striking and obvious demographic trend in Ireland has been the continuous decline in the recorded population between the late 1840s and 1961 or thereabouts. There is evidence that this trend has been reversed, or at least has levelled off in the last decade.

Another important and rapidly expanding use of census data is concerned with *sample surveys*. In general, the aim of sample surveys is to make predictions or test hypotheses about a population on the basis of a (usually very small) sample drawn from that population. A well-known example is public opinion ' polls which attempt to predict election results on the basis of the voting intentions of a small sample of the electorate. For effective results, it is obviously important that a sample should be representative, in some defined sense, of the population from which the sample is drawn. For example, a survey of incomes which was based solely upon a sample of Dublin professional men, or of Tipperary farmers, could not be used to infer anything about incomes in the country as a whole. For this particular purpose, we would require the sample to include representatives of different groups within the population; which groups, and in what proportions they should be represented, would require additional information, including the kind of data contained in the census. In this sense, the census provides a profile or framework upon which the design of the sample is based. Thus, if the census shows that 25 per cent of the labour force work in agriculture, we may wish to design the sample so that 25 per cent of the sample respondents work in agriculture.

The need to conduct sample surveys arises because it is seldom feasible or even desirable (because of time and cost) to interview every unit in a given population. Usually, social or economic inquiries involve a sample of the population — often much less than one per cent — and the results of the sample inquiry are used to infer characteristics of the whole population. The census is an invaluable source for determining the size and composition of such samples. For example, if we had a group of patients with a certain illness and wanted to find out whether these people differed from the rest of the population in their diet, occupation or social background, we should need to select for comparative purposes a sample of persons representative of that population. Census data provide a great deal of information which is needed for survey work of this kind, albeit a little out-of-date since the structure of the population changes continuously. As a somewhat different example, a television manufacturer may be interested in comparing the geographic distribution of his sales over some recent period with the corresponding distribution of households given in the census. Almost all national market research studies draw upon census data as a frame of reference. Some terms and concepts used in sample surveys are described in chapter 10, but the preceding paragraphs indicate the importance of the census for fieldwork in the social sciences and business.

So far, three interconnected uses of census data have been identified; as the raw material for describing various characteristics of a society at a particular moment; as a means of analysing trends in the structure of the population; and as a basis for a wide range of studies involving the use of sample survey techniques. In addition, census data are often used to forecast certain characteristics of our society: the total population, the number of persons over sixty-five, the population of particular counties, the potential labour force, and so on. Studies of this kind can be viewed as extensions of time series analysis into the future, in which future events are predicted on the basis of past and current trends. Aspects of such predictions will be referred to in the next chapter, but one point to stress here is that projection of time series trends into the future is notoriously risky. In the nineteen fifties, a number of apocalyptic books and articles[3] were written which suggested that in a few years time the Irish resident population would be negligible. In part, these dire predictions were based on the currently high figures for emigration, but they were influenced also by the continuous historical downwards trend in the population of Ireland over the preceding century, and were to some extent extrapolations of that trend. However, simple extrapolations of past trends are likely to go wrong unless we also try to identify and predict the real causes underlying them: economic growth or lack of it, changes in technology, in productivity, in communications, and so on.

1.3 RECENT CENSUS DATA

To acquire a basic understanding of and ability to use demographic data, there is no substitute for careful study of the census volumes; better still is to pose some problem which requires reference to and manipulation of the basic census data. Before using these data for any purpose, it is important to read the introductory notes and definitions which preface each volume. To give some indication of their nature and scope, this section will describe briefly recent Irish census data.

3. For example, John A. O'Brien (ed.), *The Vanishing Irish*, London: W.H. Allen, 1954.

The results of the 1961 census were published in nine volumes (excluding the brief *Preliminary Report*). These were:

Volume I	(1963)	Population, Area and Valuation of each District Electoral Division and of each larger Unit of Area
Volume II	(1963)	Ages and Conjugal Conditions (classified by areas only)
Volume III	(1963)	Occupations (of Males and Females in each Province, County, County Borough, and in each Town of 5,000 and over population)
Volume IV	(1964)	Industries
Volume V	(1964)	Occupations (classified by ages and conjugal conditions)
Volume VI	(1964)	Housing and Social Amenities
Volume VII	(1965)	Part I – Religions
		Part II – Birthplaces
Volume VIII	(1965)	Fertility of Marriage
Volume IX	(1966)	Irish Language

Volumes I and II contain the basic material of any census: the size and distribution of the population by area, sex, age and conjugal condition. The smallest unit of area for which population data are published in Ireland is the district electoral division (or ward) of which there were 3065 in the state at the time of the 1961 census. Population data for larger units of area, including electoral constituencies, urban and rural districts, counties, registrars' districts, towns and, of course, provinces, are also included. Also included, at state and province level, are time series data for marriages, births, deaths and estimated net migration between census dates.

Following the detailed area breakdown of population, Volume II analyses, by area, the sex and age composition, and conjugal condition of the population. Derived statistics here include the percentage of single males and females in each group in each area, and females per 100 males, by age-group and area. Census data for earlier years are used to show changes in the age distribution of the population.

Volumes III – V of the 1961 census are essentially concerned with economic characteristics of the population, and published data generally refer to persons aged 14 and over at the time of the census. The population aged 14 and over is further subdivided into 'gainfully occupied' and 'not gainfully occupied', the latter comprising retired persons, students and persons engaged in 'home duties' — i.e. housewives — but *not* persons out of work, who are included with the gainfully occupied.

Three main forms of classification are used in analysing the characteristics of the gainfully occupied population: occupation, industry, and employment status. Volume III of the census is primarily concerned with an occupational breakdown of the population, by area, with separate data for males and females. At the most detailed level, over 200 occupations are distinguished. Volume III also contains an analysis of the population, at county level, by social group. For this purpose, eleven different social groups are defined: farmers, farmers' relatives, and farm managers; other agricultural occupations and fishermen; higher professional; lower professional; employers and managers; salaried employees; intermediate non-manual; other non-manual; skilled manual; semi-skilled manual; unskilled manual. An appendix to Volume III lists the occupations assigned to each social group. The concept of 'social group' is, of course, imprecise, and there is an arbitrary element in the assignation of certain occupations to certain social groups. However, such a breakdown of the population is useful for various types of economic and social analysis, and is one of the taxonomic criteria used in social survey and market research work.

Volume III also contains an analysis of the gainfully occupied population, by occupation and employment status, and sex. For purposes of employment status, persons are defined as employer; own-account worker (self-employed); assisting relative; employee; apprentice; and out of work.

Volume IV is primarily concerned with the industrial distribution of the gainfully occupied population (including agricultural and service industries). Tables include classifications of the working population by industry and area, industry and occupation, and industry and employment status. For some individuals, such as farmers or coal miners, 'occupation' and 'industry' are identical or very nearly so. In most cases, however, occupation and industry are separate concepts; for example, electricians, clerks and accountants are employed over a wide range of industries.

As the title suggests, Volume V of the census analyses the socio-economic characteristics and conjugal status of different age-groups within the population. Included here are statistics of males and females in each occupation by age, conjugal condition and area; age-groups by social group and conjugal condition; males and females in each industry, by age-group. Taken together, Volumes III – V provide a detailed profile of the occupational and industrial composition of the gainfully occupied population.

The remaining volumes of the 1961 census relate to aspects of the population which are not subjects of inquiry at every census. In general, some census data may be collected only at periodic censuses, or even on a once-for-all basis. For this reason, the results of such special inquiries are usually of particular interest, and the 1961 census is notable in this respect.

Volume VI of the 1961 census contains a comprehensive analysis of housing and housing amenities, not dealt with since the 1946 census. The results of this inquiry provide valuable information on housing density throughout the country, and in individual rural and urban areas. Data collected, and derived statistics, include the distribution and average size of private dwellings (in number of rooms), number of persons per household, number of persons per room, nature of occupancy (local authority, owner-occupier, etc.), rents, availability and nature of water supply, sanitary facilities and electricity supply, and age of dwelling. The result is a highly detailed profile of the nation's housing. This inquiry is discussed at greater length in chapter 4.

Volume VII comprises two independent sections. Part I contains a breakdown of the population by religious denomination, and analyses the distribution of the population by religious denomination, county and occupation. Since ninety-five per cent of the population are recorded as 'Catholic', these data are mainly of interest in showing the distribution of the minority religious groups. Part II contains an analysis of the population by birthplace and current area of residence. Such data can be used in analysing the pattern of internal migration, and are referred to in the next chapter.

The 1961 census also included a special inquiry on fertility of marriage, which also had not been analysed since 1946. The results, published as Volume VIII in the series of census reports, are of particular interest in relation to projections and forecasts of future population, discussed in chapter 2. The basic census results include a breakdown of families by number of children born, related to duration of marriage, age of wife at marriage, and age of husband at marriage. Statistics, such as the average number of children born per hundred families, are derived from these data and can be used, in conjunction with other data, in analyses of reproduction rates and trends in total population.

Finally, Volume IX presents the result of an inquiry into the knowledge and use of the Irish language by persons aged three and over. (Again, the previous language inquiry was in 1946.) Results include numbers of Irish and non-Irish speakers by county and age-group, and number and percentages of Irish speakers in each occupational group, with separate data for males and females. More detailed information is given for the Gaeltacht (Irish-speaking) areas. These data are, of course, subjective to the extent that respondents may exaggerate (or less probably, understate) their knowledge of Irish.

As this brief description indicates, the 1961 census was comprehensive in scope, indeed more so than any census since 1946. For a wide range of research topics in social, economic and business fields, such census material provides a very important and often essential starting-point.

The 1966 census results were published in seven volumes.

Volume I	(1967)	Population of District Electoral Divisions, Towns and larger units of area
Volume II	(1968)	Ages and Conjugal Conditions (classified by area)
Volume III	(1968)	Industries
Volume IV	(1969)	Occupations
Volume V	(1969)	Occupations and Industries (classified by ages and conjugal conditions)

Volume VI   (1969)   Housing and Households
Volume VII   (1970)   Education

As the titles indicate, the content and coverage of Volumes I – V of the 1966 census are similar to the 1961 census, though there are minor changes and additions, referred to in the text of the census reports, which should be read before using the data of both censuses for comparisons. These include additional tables for the Gaeltacht and inhabited islands (Vol. I), analysis of males and females at work in cities and towns (including environs) of 1500 or more population (Vols. III – IV), and an industrial, occupational and age analysis of those recorded as out of work (Vol. V). In addition, each volume carries a commentary, with supplementary tables and derived statistics, on the principal results of each census report.

The 1966 census also includes an inquiry on housing, though it is less comprehensive than the 1961 inquiry; questions on water supply, sanitation, electricity and age of dwelling are omitted. The 1966 report (Vol. VI) also includes a form of classification of households not used in the 1961 census. For further details and a comparison of the two census reports, see chapter 4.

The novel feature of the 1966 census is a special inquiry on education, results of which are published in Volume VII of the report series. This was the first time such an inquiry had been conducted as part of the Irish census. Because of its novelty and subject-matter, the scope of the inquiry was limited to an investigation of the age at which respondents' full-time education had ceased, and the type of educational establishment attended by persons whose full-time education had ceased. Nevertheless, in conjunction with other data collected in the census, particularly age-group, area of residence, occupation and industry, the results of this inquiry provide a rich vein of information. Contents of the inquiry are described more fully in chapter 5.

The 1971 census exceeds even the 1961 census in its range of inquiry, and it is expected that at least thirteen volumes will be published, including further data on housing, education, fertility of marriage and the Irish language. Special features include information on migration, on scientific and technical qualifications, and on transport to work and car ownership.

This census also departs from traditional practice in the presentation of results: a series of forty-one *preliminary bulletins* have been published, the first thirty-seven summarising census results for each county, county borough and province, and the remaining four summarising various data for the state as a whole. In addition, information similar to that published in the county bulletins can be obtained for smaller areas (district electoral division, ward and towns of 1000 population and over).[4] In part, these preliminary bulletins are intended to compensate for the delay before the detailed census volumes are published.

As noted, summary census data are published in the annual *Statistical Abstract* of Ireland. The *Abstract* contains a brief commentary on recent trends in population and a number of tables, many of which include comparable data for earlier censuses; these provide a good starting-point for analysing trends in the level and composition of the population. The *Abstract* is an extremely useful basic reference source.

Firm estimates of total population are available only at five-year (or ten-year) intervals. For inter-censal years, estimates of total population are made by adjusting the latest known census figures to account for births, deaths and external migration. While figures for annual births and deaths can be assumed to be accurate, annual estimates of emigration are difficult to obtain because of the frequency and freedom of movement between the Republic, Northern Ireland, and Britain. Inter-censal estimates of population are therefore provisional and subject to a margin of error. Provisional estimates of total population for inter-censal years are published in the *Annual Report on Vital Statistics,* compiled by the CSO. This publication is a major reference source for vital statistics and analysis of population change, and will be discussed in the following chapter.

1.4 UK AND INTERNATIONAL DATA

The most recent UK censuses are also for 1961, 1966 and 1971. The 1961 and 1971 census were full censuses, covering everyone in the population, but the 1966 census results were based

---

4.   These are not published but can be obtained from the Central Statistics Office in the form of computer print-outs, for which a small charge is made.

on a 10 per cent sample of households (except in Northern Ireland, where a full census was taken). Use of a sample census greatly reduces collection and processing costs, and time, and sample results can be be 'grossed up' to obtain estimates of total population aggregates without much loss of accuracy. Sampling fractions of 10 per cent and 1 per cent were also used in the 1971 census for the tabulation and collection of certain types of information.

Apart from the census reports themselves, there is a variety of summary sources and official references pertaining to UK population data. A useful summary source is the *Annual Abstract of Statistics* which includes breakdowns of population by age, sex and urban/rural residence, with separate data for England, Wales, Northern Ireland and Scotland. Scottish data are also published in the *Scottish Abstract of Statistics*. Summary population data are included in the *Monthly Digest of Statistics*.

Other important sources of population statistics are the various reports of the Registrars-General for England and Wales, for Scotland and for Northern Ireland. The Registrar-General for Northern Ireland publishes weekly, quarterly and annual reports on vital statistics, and population data for Northern Ireland are included in the *Digest of Statistics* published by the Department (formerly Ministry) of Finance.

Two recent United Kingdom CSO publications which deserve special mention are the monthly *Statistical News* and the annual *Social Trends* (first published in 1970). The former contains short articles and news in brief on recent publications and current developments in official statistics, and is a very useful reference for regular users of official statistics. The latter is a more substantial publication which, as the name suggests, is concerned with the analysis of social statistics and trends. As well as articles on specific subjects (including population), it includes a large number of excellently presented tables, graphs and charts. *Social Trends* is a good example of the way in which official statistics may be used — and brought to life — in social and economic investigation.

For international data, an excellent source is the *United Nations Demographic Yearbook*. This bulky volume contains population data for each country, including time series estimates of mid-year population for each country, country populations classified by sex, age and urban/rural residence, statistics of international migration, and many tables of vital statistics (birth rates, death rates) which will be discussed in the following chapter. In addition to regular series, each year's volume contains a special subject; for example in 1970 the special subject was the size and trend of world population. Other specific subjects have been infant mortality and life expectancy.

Summary population data are also recorded in the United Nations *Statistical Yearbook* and the United Nations *Monthly Bulletin of Statistics*.

SOURCES AND REFERENCES

OFFICIAL SOURCES

(a) Ireland

Census of Population Reports, CSO (Dublin: Stationery Office)
Statistical Abstract of Ireland, annual, CSO (Dublin: Stationery Office)
Annual Report on Vital Statistics, CSO (Dublin: Stationery Office)

Census data and analyses are also occasionally published in the *Irish Statistical Bulletin* (Dublin: Stationery Office).

Other sources are listed at the end of chapter 2.

(b) UK and International

The principal official sources for the UK and international census data are mentioned in section 1.4. There are regular series of publications by the General Register Offices of England and Wales, of Northern Ireland and of Scotland, and at international level by the United Nations Statistical Office and the UN Department of Economic and Social Affairs. Population statistics are also published by the World Health Organisation, reference to which is included in chapter 2.

Amongst the numerous publications by these international

agencies, two of particular interest are the *Handbook of Population Census Methods,* Vols. I - III, (UN Statistical Office, 1965) and *Proceedings of the World Population Conference 1965,* (United Nations, 1967). Although published some time ago, the *Report of the Royal Commission on Population,* Cmd 7695, (London: HMSO, 1949) contains some excellent material on demographic analysis and problems.

A useful periodical is the quarterly *Population Studies* (Population Investigation Committee, London). The *Journal of the Royal Statistical Society* (quarterly) often contains articles on population, and at a different level so does the weekly *New Society.*

OTHER REFERENCES

A number of references on specific topics are listed at the end of chapter 2. There are several general textbooks on demography. A very good concise introductory textbook is B. Benjamin's *Demographic Analysis* (London: Allen & Unwin, 1968); at a more advanced level, P.R. Cox, *Demography,* (Cambridge: Cambridge University Press, 4th edition, 1970) is a standard reference.

CHAPTER 2

VITAL STATISTICS

STUDY of population change and its determinants forms the most important aspect of demographic analysis. Changes in population result from the interaction of three factors — mortality, fertility and migration — and these will be discussed in this chapter. Statistics relating to mortality, fertility and migration are usually referred to as *vital statistics.*

2.1 MEASUREMENT AND ANALYSIS OF MORTALITY

The simplest measure of mortality is the *crude death rate,* defined as the number of deaths per thousand of the population in any period (usually a year). This can be expressed as

$$\frac{\text{annual number of deaths}}{\text{mean population}} \quad x \quad 1000$$

Since population varies slightly throughout the year, the denominator of this ratio is an average of the beginning and end-year populations.

Separate crude death rates can be calculated for males and females, for provinces and counties, and for other sub-groups in the total population, including particular age-groups, to which we refer below. The denominator of the ratio above would then refer to the mean population of the particular sub-group, or area, of interest.

For analytical purposes, crude death rates are of limited usefulness and may be misleading if used for comparisons. For example, country A may have a higher crude death rate than country B simply because, at the time of the comparison, the former had a higher proportion of elderly people; in A the death rate in each age-group may be lower, and the average expectation of life higher. It would be wrong to conclude, simply by comparing crude death rates, that B's population is healthier or enjoys a higher level of medical care than A's. Comparisons must take into account the age distribution of the population. In addition, crude death rates are also affected by longevity, trends in birth rates, and the sex composition of populations (females generally have a longer expectation of life than males, and, usually, separate death rates for females and males are calculated).

A way of neutralising the effect of age distribution on the overall crude death rate is to calculate separate death rates for each age-group in the population. These are called *age-specific death rates*, defined as

$$\frac{\text{number of deaths in specific age group}}{\text{mean population of specific age group}} \quad x \quad 1000$$

Corresponding age-specific death rates for different populations can then be compared. These rates are also influenced by age composition *within* each age-group, but provided that the age (class) intervals are fairly narrow, the influence of age distribution can be considered negligible. Five-year age-groups are commonly used.

Crude death rates (annual and quarterly) for Ireland are published in the *Irish Statistical Bulletin*, the *Quarterly Report on Births, Deaths and Marriages and on Certain Infectious Diseases* (hereafter referred to as the *Quarterly Report*), the *Annual Report on Vital Statistics*, and the annual *Statistical Abstract*.

Table 2.1 records age-specific and crude death rates for males and females in Ireland in 1970.

Note that the age-specific death rate for males exceeds the age-specific death rate for females in every age-group. Note also that the 'All ages' death rate is, in fact, the crude death rate. Age-specific death rates represent a breakdown of the crude death rate by age-group.

A more complex, but for many purposes a superior measure of mortality is the so-called *life table death rate* or its inverse, the *mean expectation of life*. Details of the construction of life tables and measures derived from them are discussed else-where [1] and will not be reproduced here *in extenso,* but the idea can be simply summarised.

Table 2.1   **Death rates for Males and Females per 1000 of the corresponding population, classified by age-group, 1970**

Age at death	Females	Males
Under 5 years	4.32	5.12
5 - 9 years	0.34	0.41
10 - 14 "	0.29	0.42
15 - 19 "	0.50	0.82
20 - 24 "	0.52	1.15
25 - 34 "	0.68	1.21
35 - 44 "	2.00	2.66
45 - 54 "	5.11	7.62
55 - 64 "	12.73	20.71
65 - 74 "	32.93	52.44
75 years and over	111.52	135.90
All ages	10.40	12.47

Source: *Statistical Abstract 1970-71*

Suppose we postulate 100000 male births at a particular time, say January 1 of year 0. This is called a *cohort* of births. We now subject this hypothetical cohort to predetermined age-specific death rates as the cohort passes through each age-group. Thus, at the end of year 0, a certain number of the cohort will be assumed to have died as a result of infant mortality.

At the end of year 1 the cohort will be further reduced, and at the end of seventy years a high proportion of the cohort will be dead. Eventually the whole cohort will be dead. It is then a

1. James McGilvray, *Irish Economic Statistics* (Dublin: Institute of Public Administration, 1969).

relatively simple matter to calculate the total number of years lived by the cohort, and hence (by dividing this total by 100000) to calculate the average number of years lived by members of the cohort. This average is called the *mean expectation of life at birth*. For example, if the mean expectation of life at birth is given as 67.2 years, this means that the average life span, or average age at death of members of the cohort was 67.2 years.

The mean expectation of life is a hypothetical measure and its value is clearly dependent on the age-specific death rates used to reduce the cohort as the cohort passes through each age-group. By using the most recently available age-specific death rates for different countries or areas, estimates of the mean expectation of life can be derived and used for comparing mortality conditions. If the mean expectation of life in country A is lower than in country B, this implies that mortality conditions in A are less favourable. Age-specific mortality rates in A may be higher at all ages, though this will not be necessarily the case. A number of qualifications must be applied to comparisons of this kind, but these will not be pursued here. Being a hypothetical measure, the expectation of life, unlike the crude death rate, is independent of the actual age distribution of the population at a given time.

The mean expectation of life may also be expressed as a death rate, called the *life table death rate* or *true death rate*. It can be shown that this rate is the reciprocal of the mean expectation of life. For example, if the mean expectation of life at birth is expressed (in years) as e_0, then the life table death rate per thousand population is

$$\frac{1}{e_0} \quad x \quad 1000$$

Life tables for Ireland, for males and females, and special life tables for urban districts, are periodically published in census of population reports, and abridged life tables are published in the *Statistical Abstract*. For a given cohort of 100000 births, these tables show (a) the expected number of survivors at each age, and (b) the expectation of life of the survivors at any age. To quote an example (*Statistical Abstract 1969*, table 28):

of 100000 male births, 88909 are expected to survive to the exact age of 50; the expectation of life of these survivors at age 50 is a further 23.50 years. From the same table, the male expectation of life at birth is 68.13 years, while for females it is 71.86 years. In general, female expectation of life is greater than male, particularly in developed countries.

The age-specific death rates used in life tables are usually the actual rates for a recent year or an average of the actual rates for two or three successive years. The Irish life tables referred to above used average specific mortality rates for 1960-63. These rates are liable to change, and predictions of life expectancy are therefore subject to qualification. The most recent set of Irish life tables, based on the 1966 census and mortality experience for 1965-67, were published in the *Statistical Bulletin* of March 1972. In less developed countries, age-specific mortality rates have been falling sharply, so that the most recent figures may significantly underestimate the actual life expectancy of current populations. For this and similar reasons, life tables require careful interpretation.

Life tables and other measures of mortality are also used to study mortality conditions amongst specific sub-groups in the population, e.g. social classes, occupations, industries and geographical areas, and also in analyses of mortality by cause. These types of application are discussed in chapter 3. Such analyses frequently make use of so-called 'standardised' mortality rates. Standardised rates are used in Ireland to calculate and compare the mortality conditions in different counties and urban areas. As with life tables, the object is to derive measures of mortality which eliminate the effects of different age distributions in the groups being compared.[2] For instance, comparing the crude death rates for County Dublin and County Mayo may give a misleading impression of relative mortality conditions, for the same reasons that the international comparison of crude death rates can be deceptive. If County Mayo has a higher proportion of elderly people in its population, its crude death rate may exceed that of County Dublin, even if Mayo's age-specific death rates are lower at every age. One way of dealing

2   For a brief description of how these rates are calculated, see *Irish Economic Statistics*, chapter 1.

with this is as follows. Age-specific death rates for Mayo are applied to a 'standard' population (e.g. the total population of Ireland at the last census), and from this a hypothetical number of deaths and a crude death rate are calculated for the standard population. This exercise is then repeated using County Dublin's age-specific death rate. Since the same 'standard' population is used in both cases, the effect of different age distributions is removed, and a comparison of the resulting 'standardised' crude death rates reflects relative mortality conditions in the two counties. Other types of standardised mortality measures are also available.

Finally, there are a number of other mortality measures which are of special interest to demographers, social scientists and health care specialists. These include the *infant mortality rate*, the *neo-natal mortality rate*, the *stillbirth rate*, the *perinatal rate*, and the *maternal mortality rate*.

The infant mortality rate is defined as the number of deaths of infants under 1 year per thousand annual live births. The neo-natal mortality rate is defined as the number of deaths of infants under four weeks old per thousand annual live births, and is therefore a component part of the overall infant mortality rate. In fact, a large proportion of infant deaths occur in the four weeks after birth and are often ascribed to pre-natal influences, such as congenital malformation, while deaths in the subsequent eleven months or so can more often be attributed to environmental factors. This is the reason for separately identifying the neo-natal component of infant mortality. For example, in 1971 the Irish infant mortality rate was 18.0 per thousand births, of which 12.2 per thousand comprised neo-natal mortality. This proportion has remained roughly constant in recent years, even though the overall infant mortality rate has fallen sharply.

The stillbirth rate is defined as the ratio of annual still-births[3] to total annual (live plus still) births. The perinatal mortality rate is measured as the ratio of stillbirths *plus* deaths of infants within seven days of birth to total annual (live plus still) births. (All these ratios are expressed as rates per thousand). Stillbirths and early neo-natal deaths commonly have a similar

---

3. 'Stillbirth' is defined as foetal death at or over 28 weeks gestation.

aetiology, and the perinatal rate is regarded as an index of the quality and availability of obstetric care. Note also that the perinatal rate avoids the often difficult problem of distinguishing exactly between a stillbirth and an infant who dies almost immediately after birth.

The maternal mortality rate is defined as deaths attributed to puerperal causes per thousand live births (or sometimes, live plus stillbirths).

Comparisons of these rates between countries show tremendous variations. For instance the 1969 infant mortality rates for Finland, Italy and Mexico were 14.0, 30.3 and 68.4 respectively, and similar variations are shown for other rates. Taken singly or together, they provide useful and important indices of relative levels of health care and social welfare provisions in different countries. Dramatic falls in these rates have been amongst the most notable developments in the less developed countries over the past two decades. Since birth rates have declined by much less (if at all), a consequence has been 'population explosions' in many of these countries.

Infant, neo-natal and maternal mortality rates are published in the *Statistical Abstract* and in the *Quarterly Report*, which also includes infant and neo-natal mortality for each county and principal town. The *Annual Report* includes detailed statistical analyses of infant and late foetal (stillbirth) mortality, including breakdowns of mortality by cause, age of mother and number of previous children born. Perinatal and maternal mortality statistics are also published.

2.2 MEASUREMENT AND ANALYSIS OF FERTILITY

Analysis of fertility concerns the rate at which a population adds to itself by births, and measures of fertility therefore relate births to population. The simplest such measure is the *crude birth rate*, defined as

$$\frac{\text{annual births}}{\text{mean population}} \quad x \quad 1000$$

Annual crude birth rates for Ireland are published in the *Annual Report* and in the *Statistical Abstract*.

A more useful measure of fertility, because it is related solely

to the population 'at risk', is the *general fertility rate*, defined
as

$$\frac{\text{annual births}}{\text{female population of child-bearing age}} \quad \text{x} \quad 1000$$

This measure eliminates that section of the population not at
risk, and hence is a better measure for comparative purposes
than the crude birth rate. In any year, however, the value of
the general fertility rate will be influenced by the age distribution of the female population at risk (the child-bearing age
span is usually taken as 15-49). For comparative purposes,
we may wish to eliminate this effect, and do so by a method
similar to that used for mortality analysis in life tables. Predetermined specific fertility rates for each age are applied to a
cohort of (say) 1000 females as they pass through the child-
bearing ages. The total number of children born to this cohort
by age 50, divided by 1000, gives the expected number of
births per person, called the *total fertility rate*. Like the life
table measures, this is a hypothetical measure based on
assumed specific fertility rates, usually based on estimated
fertility rates for the most recent census year.

Such measures of fertility are liable to considerable variation.
Specific fertility rates are affected by the proportion of women
who marry, the ages at which people marry and the duration of
marriage, social attitudes towards family size and contraception,
the urban/rural balance of population and other social and
economic factors. More complex measures of fertility have been
devised,[4] which try to account for some of these influences,
but while these are often useful in analysing present patterns
of fertility, they are not very useful for predictive purposes,
since these measures also are subject to changes which are
difficult to forecast in direction and magnitude.

Specific fertility rates for Ireland are published in the *Annual
Report*, and table 2.2 reproduces some of these data. In
column two rates are based on the ratio of births to the total
female population in each age-group, while in column three the
rates (exclusive of illegitimate births) are based on the number

4. See B. Benjamin, *Demographic Analysis* (London: Allen & Unwin, 1968), Chapter
5.

of *married* females in each age-group. The final figure in column two is the general fertility rate as defined above. Total fertility rates are not published, though such rates may be estimated from the data provided.

Table 2.2 **Age-specific fertility rates: Births per 1000 women in each age-group, Ireland 1971**

Age of mother at maternity	Total births per 1000 women	Legitimate births per 1000 married women
15 - 19	19.0	678.7
20 - 24	149.6	457.3
25 - 29	242.6	349.0
30 - 34	199.5	248.0
35 - 39	131.1	160.0
40 - 44	46.4	58.4
45 - 49	3.3	4.2
Total 15 - 49	107.3	195.1

Source: *Annual Report on Vital Statistics, 1971*

For more extensive information on patterns of fertility the most important sources are the special census inquiries referred to in the previous chapter. These inquiries were conducted as part of the 1946, 1961 and 1971 censuses. The basic information collected comprised duration of present marriage, and number of children born alive to present marriage.[5] Published analyses of the results include a classification of families by number of children born, bivariate classifications of families by number of children born and duration of marriage, by duration of marriage and age of wife at marriage, by age of wife and age of husband at marriage, and certain derived measures such as average number of children per hundred families. Distributions of this kind form the basis for analyses of fertility and, usually in conjunction with other data, for estimates of trends in total fertility and population projections.

5. Widows and single women were excluded from the inquiry.

As stated above, the observed pattern of fertility over any short interval of time is the result of a complex of factors. It is difficult to assess the significance of each of these factors and their interaction. For instance, age-specific fertility rates in Ireland are comparatively high in the upper age-groups. Similarly, the average age at marriage is comparatively high in Ireland. If the average age at marriage declines, will age-specific fertility rates in the upper age-groups also decline? Such a hypothesis assumes that the main effect of younger marriage would be on the timing rather than on the number of children born, and further assumes the exercise of some control over fertility. The contrary hypothesis would imply that, as average age at marriage declined, total fertility would rise [1].

Again, observed fertility (and nuptiality) patterns at any time reflect the experience of different generations or cohorts, and it may be quite misleading to assume that (current) age-specific fertility rates in the age-group 30-34 will apply to the present generation of females in the age-group 20-24 in ten years time. Recall that a similar problem applies to the interpretation of specific mortality rates in life tables.

Thus, analysis of fertility requires consideration of such parameters as nuptiality (marriage) rates, age of wife at marriage, duration of marriage and average size of family. From these data, we can try to infer something about the effects of age at marriage and duration of marriage on fertility, and inter-generational differences in fertility. The 1946, 1961 and 1971 special inquiries provide the data required for these kinds of analyses. In addition, a considerable volume of data on nuptiality is published each year in the *Annual Report*, including analyses of marriages by age of groom and age of bride, by area and by social group.

Estimates of future mortality and fertility rates are used to predict trends in total population. In developed countries at least, trends in specific mortality rates are sufficiently predictable to rule out serious errors in population forecasts caused by differences between actual and forecast mortality. Estimates of future fertility, however, are liable to substantial error and medium- to long-term forecasts of population are highly sensitive to changes in fertility rates. Frequently, population forecasts are drastically revised as more recent information on trends in fertility comes to light, but there is no guarantee that these trends will be maintained.

The simplest acceptable method of forecasting population can be derived from the total fertility rate. The latter purports to measure the number of children born to a cohort of (say) 1000 females throughout the at-risk age span. To convert this to a measure of population replacement, it is convenient to consider only the estimated number of *female* children born to the cohort; this will be slightly less than half the total fertility rate, since the probability of a male birth is slightly greater than one half. The result, the estimated number of female children born to a cohort of 1000 females, is called the *gross reproduction rate*. Utilising age-specific mortality rates to account for the probability that not all females will live to age 50, and not all female children born will reach 15, we obtain the *net reproduction rate*.

Under constant mortality and fertility conditions, the net reproduction rate tells us whether the female population is replacing itself, and, *ceteris paribus*, indicates the underlying trend in total population. A rate equal to unity (i.e., one thousand female children per thousand females) indicates that the population is just replacing itself and is therefore constant in size, even though short-term movements in population may give a quite different impression.

The net reproduction rate can be seen as a measure of cohort replacement, or the extent to which a generation of females reproduces itself. Thus a value of 1200 for the reproduction rate implies a ratio of 1200 to 1000 females from one generation to the next. Given the length of a 'generation' in years, the measure can be converted to an annual rate by means of the formula,

$$(1 + r)^n = R$$

where n is the length of a generation, in years, R is the net reproduction rate and r is the annual rate of increase, which may be calculated from the above formula given the values of R and n. Under constant mortality and fertility conditions, r measures the annual trend rate of change in population. However, the assumption of constant fertility rates is so unlikely that any calculated value of r (sometimes referred to as the *true rate of natural increase*) cannot be treated very seriously as a *forecast* of population trends. At best, the measure can be interpreted as a hypothetical *projection* based on assumed mortality and fertility conditions. (In a forecast, one tries to predict what will actually happen; a projection is unconditional and carries no such implication.)

Currently-used methods of making population forecasts or projections are too complex to be discussed in detail here. In general, they are based on cohort analyses, and utilise census data on age at marriage, duration of marriage, year of marriage and similar data, as well as specific fertility and mortality rates. Reference is made to population projections in the next section, following a discussion of migration statistics.

Apart from census material, statistics relevant to fertility are published in the *Statistical Bulletin,* the *Statistical Abstract* and the *Quarterly Report,* while the most important source is the *Annual Report on Vital Statistics.*

2.3   MIGRATION

The third factor affecting changes in the level and composition of the population is migration. Over any given time period, the difference between births and deaths gives the *natural increase* in population. This may be expressed, for instance, as

$$\frac{\text{annual births - annual deaths}}{\text{mean population}} \quad x \quad 1000$$

giving the annual rate of natural increase. When net migration (immigrants *less* emigrants) is added to this, we have the total increase in population over any given period. Net migration may also be expressed as a rate per thousand, and thus we have rate of total increase = rate of natural increase *plus* rate of migration.

Any or all of these rates may be negative, though it is unusual for the rate of natural increase to be negative (implying that the death rate exceeds the birth rate). However, certain countries have been traditionally net exporters of people, including Ireland. Indeed for many years the rate of net emigration from Ireland exceeded in numerical magnitude the rate of natural increase, with the result that the rate of total increase was also negative. In recent years the rate of net emigration has fallen, and total population has increased. Recent statistics of passenger traffic actually suggest a small net *immigration* to Ireland.

In the absence of detailed checks and controls over migration, details of the level and composition of emigration and immigration are difficult to obtain. The most reliable sources of information are the censuses of population, which give estimates of total population at specific dates. In conjunction with inter-censal statistics of births and deaths, these data can be used to calculate *net* external migration between census dates. Insufficient information is available to calculate gross migration, though for the period 1961-1966 estimates of gross migration from Ireland to the UK, based on the UK census for 1966, were made by Walsh [16]. The 1971 Irish census also included a question on usual residence one year prior to the census date, which provided information on gross inflow from outside the state during that twelve-month period. Some results of this inquiry have been published in Census Bulletin No. 40.

Annual estimates of net external migration can be made from the estimates of external passenger movements published in the *Statistical Abstract*. The annual net movement inward or outward could be taken as an approximation to net migration, though of course these figures include 'temporary' as well as 'permanent' movements, and the data themselves are subject to unknown, and possibly substantial, margins of error. However satisfactory in principle, there are serious doubts about the reliability of net passenger movements as a proxy for net migration.[6]

Some limited information on the sex, age, occupation and area of former residence of emigrants is published in the *Statistical Abstract*. This is based on information collected from persons applying for new passports before leaving for permanent residence or employment abroad. These persons form only a small proportion of emigrants, and, as a sample of all emigrants, are almost certainly biased towards those who emigrate to countries other than the UK. For this and other

6. See for example B.M. Walsh, 'Some Irish Population Problems Reconsidered', ESRI Paper No. 42, 1968.

reasons, this group cannot be regarded as a representative sample of all emigrants.

For purposes of population forecasts or projections (as well as for other reasons) details of the number, age and sex of emigrants are important. As explained above, estimates of net migration can be obtained by combining successive census data with inter-censal statistics of births and deaths. For example, taking as a starting-point the recorded population at the time of the 1961 census, adding to this the recorded number of births between this date and the date of the 1966 census, and subtracting the recorded number of deaths over the same period, we arrive at an estimate of what the population would have been at the 1966 census, in the absence of any external migration. Comparing this figure with the actual recorded population in 1966 yields an estimate of *net* external migration during the period 1961-66. Separate estimates can be made for males and females.

Estimates based on this method of calculation, and derived measures such as the average annual rate of net migration and the ratio of female to male emigrants, are published in the reports of the census of population. The census reports also include estimates of net migration by county, using the same method with respect to county populations, recorded births by county of residence of mother, and recorded deaths by county of residence of the deceased. The county figures, however, include migration to and from other places within the state, as well as migration without the state. We return to these estimates below.

A similar method can be used to estimate the age distribution of emigrants. Suppose the two census dates are five years apart. Then we could take as 'benchmark' data the population of each 5-year group at the first census date; each age-group population minus deaths of persons included in that population, would then form the hypothetical population of the next 5-year age group at the second census date (for the 0-4 age group, *birth* less deaths). Finally, comparison of hypothetical with actual recorded age-group populations yields an estimate of net external migration by age.[7] In this way estimates of the number

7. See, for example, Volume II of the 1966 census.

age and sex distribution of emigrants can be obtained for a complete inter-censal period, though it should be remembered that these are net figures which may conceal substantial two-way movements.

Reference to estimates of net migration by county leads to a brief consideration of internal migration. Quantitatively this is a more important phenomenon than external migration, and has equally important implications; for instance in relation to policies on industrial location, urban development, transport, and other infrastructure services. It may also bear on trends in total population, though in a less obvious way than external migration.

Such information as there is about internal migration (apart from special surveys for research purposes) derives once again from the census of population. Reference has been made to the published estimates of county net migration, which, however, merely record the net flow into or out of each county between census dates. While the total of county net migration equals national net external migration, the individual county figures do not distinguish between migration to and from other places within the state, and migration to and from other countries. Nevertheless, examination of these data gives some indication of the direction of internal migration flows.

A further source in the census reports are the periodic analyses of population by birthplace and current area of residence, the two most recent being for 1961 and 1971. For a given census year, these data provide a measure of the magnitude and direction of internal migration, and for two census years can be used to estimate approximately the flow of internal migration over a specific period.[8] Further information on internal migration is also available from the information on usual residence one year ago collected in the 1971 census.

Unlike external migration, patterns of internal migration are not of such obvious relevance to measures of natural increase or trends in the total population. However, changes in demographic structure — for instance in the urban/rural balance of population, and occupational structure — are known to be

8. For a detailed discussion and analysis of internal migration, using 1946 and 1961 data on birthplaces, see R.C. Geary, J.G. Hughes, and C.J. Gillman, 'Internal Migration in Ireland', ESRI Paper No. 54, 1970.

associated with differences in marriage and fertility patterns (and also mortality), and in turn these changes are often linked to internal migration. Whether as a cause or consequence of other demographic changes, internal migration is relevant to considerations of trends in population.

For populations in which migration is an important and prevailing feature, forecasts of future population are more hazardous than usual. This is particularly so since a substantial proportion of migrants are drawn from younger age-groups.

Estimates for future population (whether expressed as forecasts or simply as projections) are based upon a range of assumptions about trends in mortality, fertility and external migration; in turn these assumptions — especially those related to fertility and migration — rest upon a variety of predictions and guesses about patterns of marriage, attitudes to family size and family planning, and economic circumstances. In less developed countries, it is somewhat easier to generalise about trends in population, because the predominant influences are primarily medical care facilities and subsistence-level living standards, and future developments in these areas can be predicted with greater confidence. In more developed countries, however, the determinants of fertility patterns are hard to identify and difficult to predict.

Population projections for Ireland for 1966, 1971, 1976 and 1981 were published in the *Irish Statistical Bulletin,* June 1965. Mortality rates and fertility rates are based on life tables for 1960-62 and fertility rates over the same period, though an upward trend in the proportion of married females was assumed. A declining rate of net emigration was assumed. Based on these assumptions, and the 1961 population as starting-point, projections of population by five-year age-groups were made for the years mentioned. The projections for total population in 1966 and 1971 were 2.872 million and 2.974 million respectively, compared with actual (recorded) populations of 2.884 million and 2.978 million, in the 1966 and 1971 censuses.

Population projections for five-year intervals up to 1996, based on 1966 census data, are contained in a paper by Knaggs and Keane [8]. These population projections are also broken down by county, and the paper provides a lucid and succinct explanation of the methodology used.

2.4   UK AND INTERNATIONAL SOURCES

A number of the most important sources were listed in the previous chapter. For the UK, a good summary source is the *Annual Abstract of Statistics*; data for Scotland and Northern Ireland are also published separately in the *Scottish Abstract of Statistics* and the *Digest of Statistics,* respectively. Data with commentary, and occasional articles on aspects of vital statistics appear in *Social Trends.* For more detailed information and analyses, the annual reports of the Registrars-General for England and Wales, for Scotland and for Northern Ireland are the principal sources.

For international data on mortality, fertility and migration, the most comprehensive source is the United Nations *Demographic Yearbook.* As explained in chapter 1, each issue of the *Yearbook* includes a special subject related to a particular aspect of demography; in 1966 and 1967, for example, the special subject was mortality statistics, and included detailed analyses of foetal deaths and perinatal mortality. Summary data are also published in the UN *Monthly Bulletin of Statistics* and *Statistical Yearbook.* Special publications on population and vital statistics are also produced by the United Nations Department of Economic and Social Affairs, mentioned in the note on references at the end of the previous chapter.

SOURCES AND REFERENCES

OFFICIAL SOURCES

(a) Ireland

Quarterly Report on Births, Deaths and Marriages and Certain Infectious Diseases, CSO (Dublin: Stationery Office)

For additional sources see the list at the end of chapter 1.

(b) UK and International

See section 2.4 and the list of sources at the end of chapter 1.

OTHER REFERENCES

This is not intended to be a comprehensive bibliography. However, it includes most of the important studies of Irish population problems, at least in recent years.

The most comprehensive demographic survey of Ireland is included in the *Reports of the Commission on Emigration and other Population Problems* (Dublin, 1954).

Since the mid-1960s, there has been a steady flow of publications on problems and characteristics of Ireland's population, most of which have emanated from the Economic and Social Research Institute (ESRI), or have been published in the Institute's *Economic and Social Review*.

[1] James Deeny, *The Irish Worker. A Demographic Study of the Labour Force in Ireland* (Dublin: Institute of Public Administration, 1971)

[2] Garret FitzGerald, 'Demographic Development', *The Irish Times*, 23-24 April 1974

[3] R.C. Geary, J.G. Hughes, and C.J. Gillman 'Internal Migration in Ireland', ESRI Paper No. 54, 1970

[4] D. Hannan, *Rural Exodus: A Study of the Forces Influencing the Large-Scale Migration of Irish Rural Youth* (London: Chapman, 1970)

[5] B. Hutchinson, 'Observations on Age at Marriage in Dublin, related to Social Status and Social Mobility', *Economic and Social Review*, II, 2, 1971

[6] B. Hutchinson, 'Social Status in Dublin: Marriage, Mobility and First Employment', ESRI Paper No. 67, 1973

[7] N. Johnson, 'Migration Patterns in Dublin County Borough', *Economic and Social Review*, V, 2, 1974

[8] J.F. Knaggs, and T. Keane, 'Population Projections', *Journal of the Statistical and Social Inquiry Society of Ireland*, XXII, 4, 1971-72

[9] C.E.V. Leser, 'Recent Demographic Developments in Ireland', *Journal of the Statistical and Social Inquiry Society of Ireland*, XII, 3, 1964/65 (also ESRI Reprint Series No. 10, 1965)

[10] M.D. McCarthy, 'The 1961 Census of Population', *Journal of the Statistical and Social Inquiry Society of Ireland*, XX, 4, 1961

[11] B.M. Walsh, 'Some Irish Population Problems Reconsidered', ESRI Paper No. 42, 1968

[12] B.M. Walsh, 'An Empirical Study of the Age Structure of the Irish Population', *Economic and Social Review,* I, 2, 1969-70

[13] B.M. Walsh, 'Religion and Demographic Behaviour in Ireland', with Appendix by R.C. Geary and J.G. Hughes on Migration between Northern Ireland and the Republic of Ireland, ESRI Paper No. 55, 1970

[14] B.M. Walsh, 'Ireland's Demographic Transformation 1958-1970', *Economic and Social Review,* III, 2, 1971-72

[15] B.M. Walsh, 'Trends in Age at Marriage in Post-War Ireland', ESRI Reprint Series No. 29

[16] B.M. Walsh, 'Migration to the United Kingdom from Ireland 1961-1966', ESRI Memorandum Series No. 70

CHAPTER 3

HEALTH

IT may be debatable whether or not health statistics should be included under the general rubric of social statistics, but there are good reasons for including in this book a brief description of the main sources of health statistics. The provision and administration of health care is increasingly regarded as an integral part of the range of social services provided by the state, and hence should be considered along with other services such as housing and education. Moreover, efforts by social scientists to describe communities by means of so-called 'social indicators' must necessarily lend considerable weight to indicators of the health of members of that community and the availability of health care facilities.[1] For these reasons a survey of social statistics should include reference to the main sources and uses of health statistics. This chapter, however, is mainly confined to the description of sources and measures concerned with analyses of mortality and morbidity. Statistics of the structure and financing of the health services have been omitted; these are comprehensively described by Hensey [1], though in recent years there have been substantial changes in the organisation of these services.

3.1 ANALYSIS OF MORTALITY

In the previous chapter a number of measures of mortality were

1. Economists have long been used to measures, such as national income per head (see chapter 7), as indicators of economic welfare. However this cannot adequately describe all aspects of human welfare; hence the search for other, more comprehensive or supplementary measures, of which measures of health conditions are amongst the most important.

described, including the crude death rate, which is simply the number of deaths per thousand of the population in any period. The limitations of the crude death rate led to discussion of more discriminating methods of analysis, including age-specific death rates, life tables, and standardised mortality rates. In this chapter the use of these measures, and some others, will be elaborated.

Two lines of approach can be developed, which are complementary rather than mutually exclusive. One approach is concerned with the influence of social, economic and other environmental factors on mortality, the other with the relative importance of and trends in proximate cause of death. However, the two approaches converge since in many instances cause of death or mortality risk is associated with environmental circumstances.

Simple analyses of mortality by cause of death present little difficulty.[2] As a starting-point, the number of recorded deaths in any period (e.g. a year) can be classified by cause of death. A mortality rate for each cause of death can then be calculated, as the ratio of deaths by cause to total (mean) population. Separate rates can be calculated for males and females.

These mortality rates are in effect crude death rates by cause of death, and are simply a breakdown of the overall crude death rate. An example is shown in Table 3.1, which classifies deaths by cause of death, and subsequently death rates by cause per 100000 population. The sum of crude death rates by cause is equal to the overall crude death rate for the population in 1970.

The classification of diseases and causes of death used in the *Annual Report* is based on the 8th Revision of the International Statistical Classification of Diseases, Injuries and Causes of Death. The code numbers recorded in the left-hand column of Table 3.1 are International Detailed List numbers and define the causes of death included within each of the principal causes of death listed in the second column. The summary grouping used in Table 3.1 is not unique; the form of grouping depends upon the purpose for which the data are to be used.

---

2. Though investigation of death certification suggests systematic errors in diagnosis and recorded cause of death. See Bourke [3].

Table 3.1   **Annual number of deaths and death rates from principal causes, Ireland 1970**

International List Nos. 8th Revision	Cause	Number	Rate per 100 000 population
010 - 019	Tuberculosis, all forms	221	7.5
Rem. 000 - 136	Other infectious and parasitic diseases	212	7.2
140 - 209	Cancer	5514	188.3
393 - 398, 410 - 429	Diseases of the heart	9904	336.4
Rem. 390 - 458	Other diseases of the circulatory system	6915	234.9
470 - 474	Influenza	704	23.9
Rem. 460 - 519	Other diseases of the respiratory system	4426	150.3
794	Senility	599	20.3
	Other diseases	3747	127.3
800 - 999	Accidents and other external causes	1414	48.0
	All causes	33686	1144.1

Source: *Annual Report on Vital Statistics, 1970*, Table XIX

Changes over time in death rates by cause have to be interpreted with care. Advances in medical research, improvements in diagnosis, and extension of health care facilities affect death certification, classification procedures and the numbers and grouping of codes, and the International Detailed List is periodically revised. Such changes affect comparisons of death rates by cause over time.

Changes in relative mortality by cause may be liable to misinterpretation for another reason. A successful campaign to eradicate tuberculosis, for example, may not have much short-run effects on death rates for other causes of death (though it is bound to have some effect), but obviously affects the *relative* importance of other causes of death. In the longer run, lower death rates for some causes will result in higher death rates for other causes — for example diseases of the circulatory system, which include cardiac failure in old age, are certain to rise as progress in health care leads to a greater life expectancy.

A further step in the analysis of mortality by cause is to classify deaths by cause and age-group. From this, age-specific mortality rates by cause can be calculated (with separate rates for males and females). This approach essentially involves a breakdown of the age-specific mortality rates described in the previous chapter, and provides a measure of the relative importance of different causes of death at different ages. This may well lead to a different emphasis on the importance of particular causes of death, than a comparison based merely on overall death rates by cause for all ages.

With age-specific mortality rates by cause available, various standardised mortality measures can be calculated. For example, 1971 age-specific mortality rates for, say, lung cancer, could be applied to the 1966 and 1961 populations, to yield 'expected' deaths from lung cancer in 1966 and 1961 — that is, the deaths from lung cancer which would have occurred in 1966 and 1961, had 1971 cancer mortality rates applied in those years. The ratios of 'actual' to 'expected' deaths from lung cancer in those years are called *standardised mortality ratios.* Usually these ratios àre multiplied by 100. As a hypothetical example, suppose we get the following results:

	1961	1966	1971
Actual deaths	6100	6500	7000
'Expected' deaths	6700	6800	7000
Ratio (x 100)	91	96	100

Actual and expected deaths in 1971 are equal because we use the actual 1971 specific mortality rates to compute expected deaths. Actual and expected deaths in 1961, and in 1966, are different because actual specific mortality rates in these years were different from (and in this hypothetical example generally lower than) the actual 1971 rates which were used to calculate expected deaths in 1961 and 1966. The ratios of actual to expected deaths in 1961 and 1966 are less than unity, and hence less than 100 when multiplied by 100. We can therefore conclude that there has been an increase in mortality from this cause, shown by an increase over time in the value of the standardised mortality ratio (SMR), from 91 to 100.[3] The important point is that the standardised mortality measure minimises the effects of differences in age distribution on the time series of mortality rates. A comparison of crude mortality rates over time may be misleading as an indicator of trends if there are notable differences in age distribution in the periods being compared. Standardised mortality ratios can be calculated for each cause of death and are useful indicators of comparative trends in mortality.

If age-specific mortality rates by cause are available for different areas of the country, standardised mortality measures can be devised to minimise the effects of area differences in age structure. For example, suppose age-specific mortality rates for tuberculosis are available for each province, as well as for the whole country. One method of standardisation is as follows. The age-specific rates for each province are applied in turn to the same 'standard' population (usually the population of the whole country) to yield estimates of the deaths from tuberculosis which would have occurred if the age-specific rates for each province had applied nationally. The number of 'expected' deaths is then expressed as a crude death rate per 100 000 of the standard population. The resulting (hypothetical) death rates are directly comparable since the same standard population has been used in conjunction with the age-specific death rates for each province. Moreover, the ratio of these estimated rates to the observed (actual) national rate (assuming the national population has been used as the standard) gives a standardised mortality ratio for each province, similar to that described for comparisons over time. The method of calculation is different, but the aim is the same — to minimise the effect of differences in age structure on mortality measures.

The preceding paragraphs have summarised two examples of standardisation. Other methods and applications are available.

_____

3. The reader will note that in this example the 1971 age-specific mortality rates have been used as the 'standard' for calculating expected deaths in each year. Alternatively, the actual age-specific rates for 1961, or 1966, or some other year, could have been used as standard. The numerical values of the SMRs would have been different, but the trend in the values of the SMRs would have been the same.

However, discussion of area comparisons of mortality by cause leads to consideration of the effects of environmental factors on mortality, and methods which might be used to analyse such effects.
Environmental factors play an important role in analysis of mortality. For example, in Ireland, and in many other countries, separate life tables are computed for urban areas, and mortality measures derived from these tables are assumed to reflect the impact of such factors as population and housing density, air pollution, greater traffic densities, etc., which are known or are assumed to affect mortality (though not necessarily always in the same direction − for instance urban dwellers might benefit through easier access to specialist medical care).
The importance of particular environmental factors may be expected to vary with the type of disease or cause of death. As a starting-point, however, it is convenient to consider mortality from all causes, and to consider how the effects of environmental factors may be analysed.
What we need to do here is to classify the population according to some criteria of (alleged) 'environmental risk' and then devise and compare measures of mortality for each class. (Of course, there is a certain element of circularity here, since our choice of criteria may be suggested by observation of different mortality experience.) An example, already referred to, is the construction of separate urban area life tables, on the assumption that the urban environment has an effect on mortality. Unfortunately, there is (as yet) no acceptable single index of environmental influence which includes all possible environmental factors, and a variety of different criteria can be, and are, used to classify populations. These include area or climate, marital status, housing density, population density, income, occupation and social status. In principle, statistical techniques, designed to identify simultaneously the influence (if any) of individual factors, can be employed, but we shall confine the discussion to cases where only one criterion of environmental risk is used at a time (though any one criterion may embrace several different risk factors, as in the case of urban populations referred to above).
A frequently-used criterion is that of occupation. Occupation of deceased is included in death registration and, in conjunction

with information on occupation recorded in the population census, can be used to estimate mortality rates for different occupation groups, at least for periods around census dates. Mortality rates thus calculated are subject to several qualifications; the occupational information recorded in the census and on the death certificate is subject to error, and it is therefore advisable to avoid too precise classifications of occupation for computing mortality rates. Secondly, there is no information on duration of occupation recorded either in the census or on the death certificate. A coal miner who retires at age fifty and subsequently becomes a school-teacher, and dies after two years in the latter occupation, will probably be recorded as a school-teacher on the death certificate. His mortality risk experience, however, has been closer to that of other coal miners than other school-teachers.

Thirdly, in interpreting such data it is important to remember that a high (low) mortality rate may not be directly attributable to a particular occupational risk, but to other circumstances associated with that occupation. For reasons of historical accident, it may be that a high proportion of the population of a particular occupation reside in an area of the country characterised by unfavourable climatic conditions, and that this factor alone causes an above-average mortality rate. It could be argued that this is part of the occupation risk, but it is not uniquely associated with the given occupation – presumably persons in other occupations also live in that area of the country. Further investigation, and more refined methods of analysis, may be required to deal with this kind of problem.

A particularly obvious example of how other factors may distort simple comparisons of occupational mortality rates is the influence of age. Recall that in chapter 2 and above, it was pointed out that comparisons of crude death rates may be misleading because of differences in age distribution in the two populations being compared. Precisely the same problem arises in comparisons of occupational mortality rates, which are simply crude death rates for specific populations defined by occupation. As might be expected, methods similar to those described in chapter 2 and earlier in this section, can be used to neutralise the influence of different age distributions. For illustrative purposes, the use of standardised mortality ratios to compare occupational mortality will be briefly described, though other methods of age standardisation are available.

Age-specific mortality rates for the whole population[4] are applied to the population of each occupation of interest, to yield a figure for 'expected' deaths in that occupation − i.e. the deaths which would have occurred if the age-specific mortality rates for each occupation were identical to the age-specific mortality rates for the whole population. The ratio of 'actual' (derived from death registration records) to 'expected' deaths in each occupation is the standardised mortality ratio. An SMR greater than unity (or greater than 100, since these ratios are usually x 100) implies a greater-than-average occupational mortality and thus a greater-than-average mortality risk. For reasons suggested above, caution is required in interpreting the results of these and similar measures, since although the measures are standardised for age, the influence of other variables is ignored. In principle we could attempt to standardise for other variables as well, but in practice this is seldom possible.

Occupational SMRs are not available for Ireland, but results for Britain show that occupations with a high SMR include miners, glassmakers, furnacemen, and publicans, while occupations with a low SMR (below 100) include teachers, civil servants, bank managers and accountants.

Subject to availability of data, there is considerable scope for analyses of the effects of environmental factors on mortality. Attempts have been made in various countries to define socio-economic groups which simultaneously differentiate a number of social and economic variables − occupation, industry and income, for example. The main problem is lack of data necessary to calculate and compare mortality rates for the groups so defined. Even if the population of each group could be determined (mainly from census data), the limited information available from death registration precludes a similarly detailed classification of deaths.

Discussion so far has centred on comparisons of overall mortality rates between different occupations or socio-economic

---

4. Unless otherwise stated, it may be assumed that male and female populations are always treated separately.

groups. In some instances, a close association has been observed between *cause* of mortality and environmental factors — examples are deaths from pneumoconiosis amongst miners, and a higher incidence of poliomyelitis amongst better-off socio-economic groups.

Observation of differences in overall mortality rates between socio-economic groups (expressed by SMRs or similar age-standardised measures) leads us to examine more closely the causes of mortality in different groups, and thus provides a synthesis between analysis of mortality by cause and analysis of mortality by socio-economic group.

Standardised mortality ratios for any cause and socio-economic group can be calculated in the following way: age-specific mortality rates by cause for the whole population are applied to the population of each socio-economic group, to yield 'expected' deaths by cause in each group. The ratio of actual to expected deaths is the SMR for each group. The method is identical to that used for calculating SMRs for all causes.

By calculating SMRs for different causes of death and socio-economic groups, a matrix can be drawn up which shows SMRs by cause and socio-economic group, and from this various inferences can be drawn regarding mortality risks in different groups in the population. As an example, table 3.2 records SMRs by cause and socio-economic group for males aged 15-64 in England and Wales in the period 1959-63.

Briefly, social class I includes professional and executive personnel, II is intermediate between I and III, III includes skilled workers and clerical workers, IV includes partly skilled workers, and V unskilled workers. These are, of course, very broad groupings.

With tuberculosis, malignant neoplasms of all types and bronchitis, there is a strong indication that mortality experience varies with social class, and that environmental factors are therefore important. Mortality from these causes is substantially below average in social classes I and II, and substantially above average in social class V. In terms of the table above, these diseases show a 'positive gradient' (SMR increases with social class index). With Hodgkin's disease and angina there is no apparent trend relation between mortality and social class, and therefore no *prima facie* case for suggesting that environment influences mortality from these diseases. In the case of nephritis, there is some evidence of a negative gradient: that is, a higher mortality incidence amongst relatively affluent groups. With infectious hepatitis, mortality declines with social class index through groups I-IV and then increases sharply. Environmental factors may be important but the aetiology is complex and further analysis is required. The Registrar-General's *Decennial Supplement* does in fact include a more detailed analysis of mortality by socio-economic class, including twenty-seven occupational categories, and calculates corresponding SMRs for married women. The idea of calculating SMRs for wives is to try to distinguish between social class and occupational risk, since, despite improvement in educational opportunity, social class and occupation are closely correlated.

Table 3.2   **Standardised mortality ratios for certain causes by socio-economic group, males 15-64**

Cause	Social Class				
	I	II	III	IV	V
Tuberculosis	40	54	96	108	185
Malignant neoplasms (all sites)	73	80	104	102	139
Hodgkin's disease	101	107	107	83	109
Infectious hepatitis	120	106	87	76	165
Bronchitis	28	50	97	101	164
Coronary disease, angina	98	95	106	96	112
Nephritis	123	96	108	89	93

Source: Registrar-General's *Decennial Supplement*, England and Wales, 1961. *Occupational Mortality Tables*. HMSO, 1971.

Mortality rates standardised for age, for all causes and for particular causes, can be calculated for sub-groups in the population other than those defined by occupation or similar socio-economic criteria. Mortality by area is an obvious example. In all cases there are problems of interpretation. Area differences in mortality, for instance, may be due to climate or similar characteristics of physical geography, but may also, or even principally, be influenced by area differences in the industrial and occupational distribution of the population. In summary, mortality is a function of many variables, and it is difficult to isolate the effects of any single variable; to do so, we need to standardise data not only for age and sex but also for all other variables except the one which is being investigated. This requires the use of more advanced tools of analysis such as regression analysis or factor analysis, descriptions of which are beyond the scope of this book.

Deaths in Ireland, classified by cause, county of residence and age-group, are published in the *Quarterly Report* and more detailed analyses are published in the *Annual Report on Vital Statistics*. Standardised death rates for all causes, and for cancer, are also published in the *Annual Report*, though the use of standardised rates is confined to the comparison of mortality between different areas of the country (counties and county boroughs). Certain statistics of deaths and death rates by cause, age and sex are reproduced in the *Statistical Abstract*, which also includes a summary life table for urban areas.[5] Comparative mortality measures for different occupations or other socio-economic groups are not published, and in general the published official sources contain very little analysis of mortality statistics.

3.2   STATISTICS OF MORBIDITY
Morbidity is defined as 'sickliness', and hence the measurement and analysis of morbidity are concerned with statistics of ill-health in all its forms. Unlike mortality, morbidity is a less precisely defined state, to be understood in relation to some concept of 'normal' health. With regard to many forms of illness or disease, of course, the deviation from a normal state of health is obvious, however broadly a normal state of health may be defined. More generally, however, the borderline between illness and health is difficult to define exactly, and must rest upon certain practical criteria for deciding what con-stitutes an abnormal condition. These criteria and their adequacy have varied through time and from country to country; in addition, the identification and recording of a morbid

5. More detailed life tables for urban areas were published in the *Statistical Bulletin*, March 1972.

condition require a point of contact between the individual concerned and the diagnostician, so that the quantity and quality of morbidity statistics depend on the level of development of health services. In fact, a wholly accurate record of morbidity conditions for a given population would require a comprehensive and continuous diagnostic record for every member of that population, an obviously unattainable goal.

It is clear that measurement and analysis of morbidity encompass a wide field, and discussion of sources and methods could extend through several chapters. This section will merely summarise some of the more important areas of morbidity statistics and the actual or potential sources of data in Ireland. In part, this circumspection is because there is rather little information about morbidity regularly published in Ireland. In the near future, however, there should be a notable increase in the volume of statistics, as a result of increased emphasis on social and preventive medicine.

Sources of information about morbidity exist as points of contact between individuals and the various persons and agencies responsible for the provision of health care. Whether or not such information becomes available, in statistical form, requires the keeping of records and subsequently the collection, processing and publication of these data by some centralised agency. In the case of mortality statistics, such a system of record-keeping, collection and processing is well-established. With certain exceptions, the collection and processing of morbidity statistics is much less established. The most obvious channels for the collection of morbidity data are general and specialist practitioners, hospitals and similar institutions. Other potential sources of information are government agencies concerned with various social services, industrial safety, road safety and the like, medical insurance records, and miscellaneous medical research organisations.

Of the major sources referred to, while practitioners keep record files, there is no established system of centralised collection and processing of data concerning the numbers of patients, examinations, diagnoses and other morbidity statistics, with certain exceptions, such as the reporting of infectious diseases. In future a limited amount of data may become available through the reports of the General Medical Services

(Payments) Board, though this covers only holders of medical cards (approximately 36 per cent of the population). In the case of hospitals, annual returns for health board (formerly local authority) and voluntary hospitals are submitted to the Department of Health, from which summary tables of in-patient statistics are prepared. For health board hospitals, the total bed complement, average daily occupancy rate, average duration of stay and average cost per patient are published. Similar though less detailed statistics are recorded for the voluntary hospitals. These data are prepared annually by the Department of Health and produced in mimeographed form under the heading of *Statistical Information on the Health Services.* This source also includes data on the supply of hospital care facilities and certain vital statistics for each of the eight health board areas, as well as some other statistics referred to below. Along with the *Annual Report on Vital Statistics*, this is the most useful general reference source for health statistics, though it contains little detailed information on morbidity. Some summary statistics on hospitals and other health care institutions are reproduced in the *Statistical Abstract.*

In the near future it is hoped that regular and detailed hospital morbidity statistics will be available through the hospital in-patient inquiry scheme organised by the Medico-Social Research Board. Under this scheme, each patient discharged from a participating hospital will have a form completed, including information about diagnosis, length of stay, age, marital status, and occupation, and all this information will be centrally processed and tabulated. (Maternity and psychiatric hospitals are excluded from the scheme, the latter because there is a separate psychiatric in-patient recording scheme.) Results of the scheme should provide a valuable and much-needed body of data on morbidity, and indeed have already been profitably utilised,[6] though the success of the scheme depends to a considerable extent on acquiring maximum coverage of hospitals throughout the country. Present arrangements for the dissemination of data derived from the inquiry appear to involve the issue of regular statistics to hospitals and consultants, and the issue on request of selected statistics for

6. See the Medico-Social Research Board Annual Report, 1972.

research purposes; it would be useful to publish various summary sets of statistics on a regular basis, either as a Medico-Social Research Board publication, or in the *Statistical Bulletin* or *Statistical Abstract*.

Statistics of episodes of infectious diseases are published in the *Quarterly Report* and the *Annual Report*. Cases of infectious diseases have to be reported to the Department of Health, and summaries of the number of cases of each type of disease are published in these reports. The data are broken down by county and county borough. Following the development of community health care and preventive programmes, mortality and morbidity from infectious diseases are now comparatively low. For many diseases, immunisation by vaccine or other prophylactic measures are available.

In the special area of mental illness, more information is available. The number of psychiatric hospital patients is relatively high in Ireland compared with other European countries, and psychiatric beds account for nearly half of the total bed complement in Irish hospitals. Mental illness is one of the main research interests of the Medico-Social Research Board. In 1963, and again in 1971, a complete census of local authority and private psychiatric hospitals was conducted, on the first occasion by the Department of Health and subsequently by the Department of Health and the Medico-Social Research Board, and continuous information about psychiatric patients is available through the national psychiatric in-patient reporting system. Results of the 1963 and 1971 censuses have been published by the Medico-Social Research Board, and include numbers and hospitalisation rates of psychiatric patients, diagnosis, length of stay, age distribution, marital status and social group. A detailed statistical analysis of admissions and discharges for the period 1965-1969, and for 1970, have been published by the Board. Prior to this, psychiatric hospital statistics were published in the reports of the inspector for mental hospitals. These and other publications are listed at the end of this chapter. A fairly comprehensive volume of data on psychiatric morbidity is therefore available.

Very little regular information has been published concerning mentally handicapped persons. The comprehensive *Report of the Commission of Inquiry on Mental Handicap* (1965)

included rough estimates of the number of mentally handicapped persons in Ireland, and details of institutions for the
mentally handicapped. A Department of Health report, 'The
Problem of the Mentally Handicapped', also included estimates
of the number of mentally handicapped, the number requiring
institutional care, and facilities available. Since then there has
been a steady improvement in available data. The *Statistical
Abstract* records the number of institutions of the mentally
handicapped (all are voluntary institutions) and total bed
capacity. *Statistical Information on the Health Services* includes
estimates of the numbers of mentally handicapped persons
catered for at residential and day centres, distinguishing
children and adults, and whether mildly, moderately or severe-
ly handicapped. A census of the mentally handicapped in residential and non-residential care was conducted in 1974 by the
Medico-Social Research Board.

Care of the aged is another area of increasing interest in
health care services. Basic statistics concerning the number and
distribution of the aged are, of course, available from the
periodic censuses of population. The elderly impose relatively
greater demands upon health and other community social
services than other sections of the population, and the provision of health care and other facilities for the aged in Ireland
was the subject of a comprehensive and excellent report *(Care
of the Aged,* report of an inter-departmental committee, Prl.
777, 1968). Specific provision for treatment and care of the
aged is provided through local authority county homes (there
is also a number of private homes for the aged), but there is
also a considerable number of elderly persons in general and
psychiatric hospitals. Statistical analysis of residents of county
homes, private homes and elderly persons in hospitals were
included in the inter-departmental committee's report, but
detailed statistics of this nature are not published regularly. In
future, however, analyses of morbidity amongst the aged should
be possible from the hospital in-patient inquiry and psychiatric
in-patient records, supplemented by data on county homes.
Systematic information on diagnosis, length of stay, age and
socio-economic conditions is essential to the planning of appropriate health care facilities for the aged. The number of county
homes and other homes for the aged, and their total bed

complement, is published in the *Statistical Abstract* and in *Statistical Information on the Health Services.* Next to psychiatric beds, beds for the care and treatment of the aged are the largest category of beds in hospitals and other institutions. Information on the health of children is to be found in a number of sources, though again little in the way of regular statistical data is published. For a general review of health care facilities for children, including statistical analyses, a useful reference is *The Child Health Services,* a report of a Department of Health study group (Prl. 171, 1967). For younger children (up to primary school age) the child welfare clinics are the principal source of information, though attendance at clinics is voluntary. For the next age-group, the schools health service examines annually up to 150 000 national schoolchildren, and submits the results to the Department of Health. In addition, health boards provide paediatric clinics for the treatment of children, who may be referred to the clinics from the child welfare clinics and schools health service as well as from general practitioners, or from elsewhere. Statistics relating to attendance at paediatric clinics were published in *The Child Health Services* report, and are included in *Statistical Information on the Health Services.* Many children, however, may receive treatment from the family doctor or from hospital outpatient departments, for which statistics are not available. For patients in paediatric hospitals, data on numbers, diagnosis, and so on, will, it is hoped, be available through the hospital in-patient inquiry. The number and bed complement of paediatric hospitals is published annually in the *Statistical Abstract.*

Statistics of mortality and morbidity arising from 'external causes', for example industrial and road vehicle accidents, are published regularly in the *Statistical Abstract.* These include a breakdown of fatal and non-fatal accidents; numbers of factory accidents notified, by industrial group; numbers of fatal and non-fatal railway accidents, distinguishing passengers, railway employees, and others; and a fairly detailed analysis of deaths and injuries in road accidents, including analyses of type of road user, type of vehicle, age and sex of victims. The *Abstract* also includes summary statistics of the number of beneficiaries in receipt of disability benefit and occupational injuries benefit, and a breakdown by county of persons in receipt of home assistance. Though these statistics arise through the operation of various social services, they are nevertheless relevant to considerations of morbidity conditions in the community. Statistics of recipients of welfare allowances under schemes administered by the Department of Health, including maintenance allowances for disabled persons and those suffering from infectious diseases, domiciliary care allowances and blind welfare allowances, are published in *Statistical Information on the Health Services*. Data relating to disability benefits, invalidity pensions, occupational injuries benefits and treatment benefits are also published in the reports of the Department of Social Welfare, and are referred to in chapter 6.

Studies of the dental services, ophthalmic services and pharmaceutical services in Ireland, by P.R. Kaim-Caudle, have been published by the Economic and Social Research Institute (see references). As these reports indicate, little is known of the state of dental health and ophthalmic health of the community, particularly amongst adults. Some data are available for children attending national schools through the operation of the schools health service, and special inquiries on dental health amongst schoolchildren were carried out by the Department of Health in 1952 and between 1961 and 1963. Some additional information on adults is also available through claims for treatment under social welfare provisions and the general medical services register. The reports of the Department of Social Welfare list the annual number of claims paid for dental treatment, optical treatment, hearing aids and contact lenses, as treatment benefits under the social insurance acts, and some data on dental, ophthalmic and aural services are included in *Statistical Information on the Health Services*. The latter also includes estimates of the number of medical practitioners, dentists and nurses per 10000 population, statistical measures which are frequently used in international comparisons of living standards.

3.3 UK AND INTERNATIONAL SOURCES

Statistics of mortality in the UK by cause and for various occupational and social groups, and of morbidity, are issued by the Office of Population Censuses and Surveys, the Department of Health and Social Security and (for Scotland) by the General Register Office (Scotland) and the Scottish Home and Health

Department. For Northern Ireland, weekly and quarterly returns, and an annual report, are issued by the Registrar-General for Northern Ireland, and summary statistics of mortality and morbidity appear in the *Ulster Year Book* and the *Digest of Statistics.* A brief list of the more important reference sources is included at the end of this chapter. Published data include, *inter alia*, mortality rates by cause and area, and standardised mortality ratios for various causes, occupations and socio-economic groups. Morbidity statistics include details of hospital discharges and length of stay for different categories of patients, out-patient attendances, age distribution of hospital patients and average lengths of stay for different categories of illness, psychiatric admissions and discharges, and some estimates of attendances at general practitioners. Statistics relating to dental and ophthalmic treatments, and pharmaceutical prescriptions are also published.

For international data, the most appropriate reference source is the World Health Organisation (WHO), which publishes regular vital and epidemiological statistics as well as a wide range of special publications. A basic WHO reference is the *World Health Statistics Annual,* and this is supplemented by the monthly *World Health Statistics Report.*

SOURCES AND REFERENCES

OFFICIAL SOURCES

(a) Ireland

Annual Report on Vital Statistics, CSO (Dublin: Stationery Office)
Quarterly Report on Births, Deaths and Marriages and on Certain Infectious Diseases, CSO (Dublin: Stationery Office)
Statistical Abstract of Ireland, CSO (Dublin: Stationery Office)
Statistical Information on the Health Services, Department of Health

(b) UK and International

Annual Report of the Registrar General for Scotland, General Register Office, Scotland (Edinburgh: HMSO)

Annual Report of the Registrar General, General Register Office, Northern Ireland (Belfast: HMSO)

Digest of Health Statistics for England and Wales, annual, Department of Health and Social Security (London: HMSO)

Digest of Statistics, annual, Department of Finance, Northern Ireland (Belfast: HMSO)

Registrar General's Decennial Supplement, England and Wales, 1961. Area Mortality Tables and Occupational Mortality Tables, Office of Population Censuses and Surveys (London: HMSO)

Registrar General's Quarterly Return, General Register Office, Northern Ireland (Belfast: HMSO)

Registrar General's Statistical Review of England and Wales, annual, Office of Population Censuses and Surveys (London: HMSO)

Report on Hospital In-Patient Enquiry, annual, Office of Population Censuses and Surveys, and Department of Health and Social Security (London: HMSO)

Scottish Health Statistics, annual, Scottish Home and Health Department (Edinburgh: HMSO)

Scottish Hospital In-Patient Statistics, annual, Scottish Home and Health Department (Edinburgh: HMSO)

Social Trends, annual, CSO (London: HMSO)

Ulster Year Book, annual (Belfast: HMSO)

Weekly Return of Births and Deaths, General Register Office, Northern Ireland (Belfast: HMSO)

World Health Statistics, annual, and monthly (Geneva: World Health Organisation)

OTHER REFERENCES

For a description of the development, structure and organisation of the health services in Ireland, the standard reference is

[1]   B. Hensey, *The Health Services of Ireland,* second revised edition, Dublin: Institute of Public Administration, 1972

A good textbook on health statistics in general and UK health statistics in particular is

[2]   B. Benjamin, *Health and Vital Statistics,* London: Allen and Unwin, 1968

A brief summary of the health services in Ireland and eligibility for various services is given in the Department of Health leaflet 'Summary of Health Services'.

In addition to the specific publications listed below, the annual reports of the Medico-Social Research Board contain an excellent summary of research work conducted by the Board.

[3]   G.J. Bourke, 'Accuracy of Death Certification', *Irish Journal of Medical Science,* II, 1 (1969)

[4]   Department of Health, *Care of the Aged,* 1968 (Dublin, Stationery Office)

[5]   Department of Health, *Outline of the Future Hospital System,* 1968 (Dublin, Stationery Office)

[6]   Department of Health, *Report of the Commission of Inquiry on Mental Handicap,* 1965 (Dublin, Stationery Office)

[7]   Department of Health, *Report of the Commission of Inquiry on Mental Illness,* 1966 (Dublin, Stationery Office)

[8]   Department of Health, *The Child Health Services,* 1967 (Dublin, Stationery Office)

[9]   Department of Health, *The Problem of the Mentally Handicapped,* (Dublin, Stationery Office)

[10]   P.R. Kaim-Caudle, *Dental Services in Ireland,* Dublin: ESRI, Broadsheet No.1, 1969

[11]   P.R. Kaim-Caudle, *Pharmaceutical Services in Ireland,* Dublin: ESRI, Broadsheet No.3, 1970

[12]   P.R. Kaim-Caudle, *Ophthalmic Services in Ireland,* Dublin: ESRI, Broadsheet No.4, 1970

[13]   A. O'Hare and D. Walsh, 'Activities of Irish Psychiatric Hospitals and Units 1965-1969', Medico-Social Research Board, 1972

[14]   A. O'Hare and D. Walsh, 'Activities of Irish Psychiatric

Hospitals and Units 1970', Medico-Social Research Board, 1974

[15] *Health Services and their future development*, 1966 (Dublin: Stationery Office)

[16] D. Walsh, 'Patients in Irish Psychiatric Hospitals in 1963 — a comparison with England and Wales', *British Journal of Psychiatry*, CXVIII, 1971

[17] D. Walsh, 'The Irish Psychiatric Hospital Census', Medico-Social Research Board, 1971

CHAPTER 4

HOUSING

HOUSING is important in several different ways. Investment in housing absorbs a substantial share of total annual investment in the economy, while personal expenditure on housing, in the form of rent, rates, mortgage payments and maintenance costs, is for most people the largest item in the family budget, apart from food. The housing sector is also a major employer of labour, and, because of the sensitivity of housebuilding activity to general economic conditions, a barometer of short-term trends in economic activity and employment.

The planning, provision and administration of housing are amongst the most important activities of local authorities. Both at national and local level, housing ranks high in social service priorities. For policy-making purposes, accurate information on housing conditions, the housing stock, housebuilding activity, and housing requirements is necessary. Fortunately, a good range of statistics on housing is available; regular statistics are issued by the Department of Local Government, supplemented by data from other sources such as the periodic censuses of housing.

The following two sections describe statistics relating to the physical supply and stock of housing, while section 4.3 summarises financial statistics.

4.1 HOUSING OUTPUT AND OTHER TIME SERIES DATA

Changes in the level and composition of the physical stock of dwellings are measured by the supply of new dwellings of various types *less* depletions caused by slum clearance, obsolescence, loss through fires, and so on. Statistics of the level and composition of the housing stock at any time are discussed in the following section. This section is principally concerned with current flow statistics of housing — that is, with gross (or net) changes in the stock of housing in particular time periods.

The most important regular source of information on housing is the *Quarterly Bulletin of Housing Statistics* issued by the Department of Local Government. (This was first published in 1968, before which the annual *Report of the Department of Local Government* was the principal source of data.) Current output of housing is represented by statistics of new dwellings completed within specified periods (fiscal years, quarters, and months of the current year), distinguishing local authority dwellings, grant-aided private dwellings, other state-aided dwellings,[1] and conversions. Conversions add to the stock of dwellings through, for example, the conversion of a large house into two or more separate dwellings. Precise estimates of the number of conversions are difficult to obtain.

Monthly data for grant-aided private dwellings completed, and for total dwellings completed, are also published in each issue of the *Statistical Bulletin* (in the section 'Economic Series'), and annual completions are also published in the *Statistical Abstract.* The *Abstract* includes a classification of local authority dwellings completed by size (number of rooms), a useful breakdown which does not appear in the *Quarterly Bulletin of Housing Statistics.* The regional distribution of house-building is recorded in the *Quarterly Bulletin* in the form of total dwellings completed in each county and in each of the four county boroughs, with separate data for local authority dwellings and other dwellings (including conversions).

It should be noted that 'dwellings completed' in any time period is not the same as housing output in the economic sense. The latter would purport to measure, in physical or value terms, the volume of housebuilding activity in any given time period, including work done on partially built dwellings. The former

1. Including houses built by the Departments of Defence, Health and Lands, the ESB, Bord na Mona, and Shannon Free Airport Development Company.

counts only dwellings completed in any period, on which work would have started in earlier periods. Given the cyclical nature of the building industry, this distinction can be quite important, particularly if the time periods considered are short. Thus a high figure for dwellings completed in a particular month may mask a relatively low level of housebuilding activity in that month. Moreover, there is often a lag between the time at which a dwelling is actually completed and its officially recorded completion, so that the figures for completions in any one month may include dwellings actually completed at some earlier date. Finally, the figures published for private 'dwellings completed with grants from the Department of Local Government' exclude, by definition, dwellings built without a grant. However, only a very small number of dwellings are built without some form of grant,[2] and estimates of the number built are apparently included with 'Conversions, etc.' in the *Quarterly Bulletin.*

The figures for total dwellings completed represent the estimated gross addition to the stock of dwellings in any time period. The net addition is, of course, less than this since each year the stock is reduced through obsolescence, re-development schemes, fires, floods and so forth. The number of depletions each year is not known; it has been suggested that a figure of 1 per cent per annum might be taken as a reasonable estimate of annual losses,[3] though comparison of the 1966 and 1971 stocks of dwellings would suggest a figure of about 0.7 per cent. Of course, the depletion rate or replacement rate may vary markedly from area to area and year to year, depending on the age structure of the housing stock, redevelopment policies, and the general state of the economy. In the period 1966 to 1971, a replacement rate of 1 per cent, equivalent to roughly 7000 dwellings per annum, would have accounted for about 55 per cent of dwellings completed (including conversions) during this period, while a replacement rate of 0.7 per cent would have accounted for approximately 40 per cent of dwellings completed. Even taking the lower figure to represent a long-run

2. In 1967-68 an estimated 200 non-grant dwellings were built, compared with 7116 grant-aided private dwellings. See *Housing in the Seventies,* 1969, Appendix IV.
3. Op.cit., page 6. See also section 4.4.

national average, the distinction between gross and net additions to the housing stock is clearly important.

The *Quarterly Bulletin* also includes estimates of 'dwellings begun or authorised' in each period (annual, quarterly and monthly), for each of the categories used in the analysis of dwellings completed. These figures provide a basis for short-term predictions of housing supply, though for this purpose housing starts only would be the more appropriate figure — dwellings authorised in one period may not be started until some later period. Figures of the level of housing starts and their trend are often used as indicators of the general level of economic activity, and are therefore of considerable interest. An upturn or downturn in housebuilding activity is often taken to presage an upturn or downturn in the economy generally, and in this respect construction activity is regarded by economists as a 'leading indicator' of short-term trends in the economy. Finally, through the operation of local government grant schemes, time series data of reconstruction grants paid (for extending, enlarging, improving and repairing houses), as well as of grants for the installation of water and sewerage facilities, are published in the *Quarterly Bulletin*. These are shown for each county and county borough, and include grants paid by other bodies such as Bord Failte and Roinn na Gaeltachta.

Housing statistics published in the *Quarterly Bulletin* and the other sources mentioned do not include any breakdown by type of dwelling, for example houses or flats, and information on other characteristics such as size is also fairly limited. Much more detailed information on these matters is available from the periodic censuses of the housing stock, which are discussed in the following section. Statistics relating to size of dwelling are also published in the *Annual Bulletin of Housing and Building Statistics for Europe* which will be discussed in section 4.4.

4.2 THE HOUSING STOCK

The series described in the previous section relate mainly to flows, or changes in the total stock of dwellings, though, as noted, depletions due to demolition, obsolescence, and so on are not deducted and the data therefore measure gross changes in the housing stock. For statistics describing the total stock of dwellings at a given time the important references are the special surveys undertaken in conjunction with the 1961, 1966, and 1971 censuses of population. (Similar inquiries were conducted in 1926, 1936 and 1946.)

These surveys were designed to provide a detailed profile of the housing stock and housing amenities throughout the country, and yielded valuable information upon which, *inter alia*, assessments of overcrowding and housing needs could be made (see references [8] and [11] for example). Results of the 1961 survey were published as a separate volume in the census series (Vol. VI, 1964, *Housing and Social Amenities*): the introduction to the report reproduces the actual questions on housing included on the census form, and these questions are reproduced here (table 4.1) to illustrate the scope of the survey. For the first time in such inquiries, information was sought on age of dwellings and electricity supply.

The published results appear in the form of tables which classify households according to one or more of the attributes or variables listed in the survey questions — for instance, a breakdown of total households according to age of dwelling. These classifications are further broken down by area, so that a fairly detailed picture emerges of the structure of the housing stock in each county and county borough. From these data a variety of summary measures, such as average size of dwelling and average number of persons per room, can be derived. Such measures are important in assessing the adequacy of the housing stock and in the formulation of national and regional housing and housing amenity programmes.

As examination of the census questions suggests, the 1961 survey was mainly concerned with the following aspects of housing:

analysis of households by size of dwelling

analysis of households by nature of occupancy (renting from local authority, owner-occupied, etc.)

analysis of dwellings by type of dwelling (house, flat, etc.)

analysis of dwelling by availability of amenities (electricity, water, sanitation)

analysis of dwellings by age

analysis of rented dwellings by amount of rent.

Table 4.1 **Questions on housing accommodation included in the 1961 Census of Population**

Q. Agricultural holdings   Area in Statute acre

State the area and rateable valuation   . . . .
of all agricultural holdings (if any)
in the State of which persons usually   Valuation (Land and
resident in the household are the   buildings)
rated occupiers. Land held under the
eleven months system or in conacre
or in commonage should be
excluded.   £ . . . .

R. Nature of occupancy of house, flat or rooms. Mark X opposite whichever term applies.

1 Rented from Local Authority (corporation, county council or urban district council).
2 Rented unfurnished, other than from Local Authority.
3 Rented furnished or part furnished.
4 Being acquired from Local Authority under Tenants Purchase or Vested Cottage Scheme.
5 Forms part of agricultural holding on which Land Purchase Annuity is being paid.
6 Owner occupied (including case of dwelling purchased by means of a loan, mortgage, etc.).
7 Occupied free of rent or at nominal rent because of nature of work (caretaker, company official, etc.).

S. Rent (For categories, 1, 2 and 3 Question R).
If the house, flat or rooms are rented, state the rent (inclusive of rates and ground rent) and strike out periods which do not apply.

$$£ \quad s \quad d \quad \begin{cases}) \text{ week} \\ ) \text{ month} \\ ) \text{ year} \end{cases}$$

T. Rooms

State the number of rooms occupied by the household (including kitchen but excluding scullery, landing, hallway, bathroom or any consulting room, office or shop).

U. Water supply. Mark X opposite whichever term applies.

    1 Cold water tap from public main, inside the building.

    2 Cold water tap from public main, outside the building only.

    3 Cold water tap piped from private source.

    4 Public well, fountain, pump or other source.

If there is a cold water tap, is it shared with another household? Write 'yes' or 'no' . . . .
Has the household use of a fixed bath? Write 'yes' or 'no' . . . . .
Has the household use of hot water tap? Write 'yes' or 'no' . . . .

V. Sanitary facilities

    (a) Mark X opposite type of sanitary facilities used by household.

        1 Flush lavatory   3 Privy or dry closet

        2 Chemical closet   4 No special facilities

(b) Are sanitary facilities shared in common with other households? ('yes' or 'no')

. . . .

(c) Has dwelling an indoor lavatory closet or privy? ('yes' or 'no')

. . . .

W.   Year in which built

Indicate the period in which the house (or other building containing the dwelling) was built by inserting X in the appropriate box. The year in which first built is required if subsequently converted or reconstructed.

1 Before 1860
2 Between 1860 and 1899 inclusive
3 Between 1900 and 1918 inclusive

4 Between 1919 and 1939 inclusive
5 Between 1940 and 1945 inclusive
6 1946 or after

X.   Electricity

Is an electricity supply laid on to the dwelling? (write 'yes' or 'no')

. . . .

Source: Census of Population 1961, Vol. VI.
(There are in addition a number of tables which relate specifically to farm dwellings.)

Certain aspects are analysed in greater detail than others. For instance, the analysis of households by size of dwelling is detailed and comprehensive, while the distribution of dwellings by type of dwelling employs a broad classification of dwelling type (house, house with shop attached, flat), which for some purposes may be considered insufficiently informative. It is important to read the introduction to the census report before using the statistics, particularly with reference to the problems of defining terms such as 'household', 'dwelling' and 'room'.

The survey carried out as part of the 1966 census was less comprehensive. Questions on water supply, sanitation, electricity supply and age of dwelling were omitted.

The 1966 survey report (Census of Population, 1969, Vol. VI, *Housing and Households*) includes classifications of households by size of dwelling, directly comparable to corresponding tables in the 1961 report, and a breakdown of households by type of dwelling also similar to that employed in the 1961 report. The remainder of the report, however, is concerned with analyses of households by characteristics not included in the 1961 census report; mainly by type of household (single person, man and wife, man, wife and one or more single children, and so on − altogether ten different types of household are defined), but also by various other characteristics including sex and age of head of household, socio-economic status of head of household (a dozen different categories are used here) and rateable valuation of dwelling. For comparative purposes, an appendix to the 1966 report recasts the 1961 data in corresponding form (the data included in this appendix were published earlier in the *Statistical Bulletin,* September 1966). A number of tables from the 1961 and 1966 survey reports are reproduced in the annual *Statistical Abstract*.

The questions on housing included in the 1971 census were similar to those in the 1961 census, including queries on water supply, sanitation, electricity supply and age of dwelling. These census reports are valuable reference sources, and, while inevitably such data become increasingly out of date for research and policy purposes, the turnover of the housing stock is low, and general characteristics of the stock are slow to change.

None of the census surveys were explicitly concerned with the physical state of maintenance of the housing stock, though certain conclusions may be inferred from the census results concerning age of dwellings and provision of amenities such as water and sanitation.[4] Information on the state of maintenance, however, should shortly be available, based on a sample survey of the housing stock which has been conducted by An Foras Forbartha.

Data on the stock of local authority dwellings are also

4. See also op.cit., chapter 1.

published in the *Quarterly Bulletin of Housing Statistics,*
which records the total number of local authority dwellings let
by the various housing authorities — county councils, county
boroughs, urban district councils and town commissioners.

4.3 FINANCIAL STATISTICS

Capital expenditure on housing — that is, expenditure on new
housebuilding and on substantial improvements to existing
houses — is financed by a combination of private and public
authorities' resources. Public authorities in Ireland contribute
approximately half of the total annual capital expenditure,
though their share has varied at different periods according to
the share of local authority housing in total housing output,
the supply of funds from the private sector, and the importance
attributed by the government to increasing housing supply.

In the last ten years or so, capital expenditure on housing has
accounted for between 17 per cent and 21 per cent of annual
gross domestic fixed capital formation, and for between 3.5 and
4.0 per cent of expenditure on gross national product, which
gives some indication of the relative importance of housing in
the economy.

The largest single component in public authorities' capital
expenditure on housing is local authority housing, but substantial assistance is provided to the private housing sector, in
the form of loans and grants by local authorities and by the
Department of Local Government. Details of annual capital
expenditure on housing by public authorities are published in
the *Quarterly Bulletin of Housing Statistics,* distinguishing
local authority housing expenditure, house purchase loans,
supplementary grants and Department of Local Government
grants to the private sector, and capital expenditure on housing
by other bodies such as the National Building Agency, Shannon
Free Airport Development Company and Roinn na Gaeltachta.
With respect to local authorities' house purchase loans, the
average value of loans paid each quarter, and a classification of
borrowers by broad income ranges, is recorded for the country
as a whole and for the Cork, Dublin, Limerick, Waterford and
Galway areas. Details of capital expenditure on housing in each
county are published in the annual *Returns of Local Taxation.*

Private capital expenditure on housing is mainly financed by building societies, assurance companies, banks and personal savings. Details of the number and value of loans approved and paid by building societies and assurance companies, and a breakdown of borrowers by income range and area, are published in the *Quarterly Bulletin.*

Current housing expenditure and receipts by public authorities may be found in the *Quarterly Bulletin, Returns of Local Taxation* and the annual *National Income and Expenditure.* The accounts presented in the *Quarterly Bulletin* are aggregate accounts for all local authorities; details for individual local authorities are published in the *Returns of Local Taxation.* By far the largest component in current expenditure is loan charges — interest on capital funds borrowed to finance local authority housing, and on loans and grants to private housing. Although where possible local authorities are urged to charge 'economic rents', receipts from rents and loan purchase annuities fail to cover loan charges, and the deficit is increased when account is taken of maintenance expenditure on local authority housing and other current outlays. Deficits are met by subsidies out of general taxation and rates, which together comprise over half the current receipts on local authorities' housing accounts. In addition, private house-owners are subsidised through rates remission on new houses and tax relief on mortgage interest payments, which is a cost to public authorities through revenue foregone.

Average weekly rents for local authority dwellings are published in the *Quarterly Bulletin*, with separate data for county boroughs, county councils and urban districts. Rents for private dwellings are not available on a regular basis, though the 1961 census included an analysis of dwellings by rent paid.

The *Quarterly Bulletin* also includes time series of average new house prices, based on loans approved by building societies, assurance companies, and local authorities. Separate data are recorded for the Cork, Dublin, Limerick, Waterford and Galway areas. From these data, trends in average new house prices can be plotted, and compared with other series on prices and incomes. Less information is available for second-hand house prices, but the *Bulletin* includes a series of average prices for the Dublin area, based on a sample (though not a random sample) of sales.

4.4   UK AND INTERNATIONAL SOURCES

Inquiries on housing conditions are regularly included in UK population censuses and, as in Ireland, separate volumes on housing are issued in the census report series. In addition the county and local authority area volumes include statistics of household composition and housing conditions. Separate reports are issued for England and Wales, Northern Ireland and Scotland. The scope of the inquiries on housing, and analyses of the results, are similar to those described for Ireland, and also provide a detailed profile of the housing stock at a given time.

A useful source for current housing statistics is the quarterly *Housing and Construction Statistics*, a joint publication of the Department of the Environment, the Scottish Development Department and the Welsh Office. It includes a considerable volume of data, including building costs and new house prices; output and new orders, by region; employment and unemployment in the industry; dwellings completed, started and under construction, by region; details of local authority housing; improvement grants, slum clearance; level and sources of housing finance; rents, and cost and supply of building materials. In addition to these regular series, each issue includes a number of supplementary tables, for example, an analysis of the number and size of firms in the construction industry, or an analysis of households by income and type of tenure (owner-occupier, etc.), based on the annual *Family Expenditure Survey*. In fact *Housing and Construction Statistics* is similar to the Irish *Quarterly Bulletin of Housing Statistics*, though more extensive in coverage.

Some of the tables in *Housing and Construction Statistics* include data for Northern Ireland, but the main source of data for Northern Ireland is the quarterly *Digest of Housing Statistics for Northern Ireland*, compiled by the Department of Housing, Local Government and Planning. Summary data are also published in the twice-yearly *Digest of Statistics*, compiled by the Northern Ireland Department of Finance.

The main series published in *Housing and Construction Statistics* are themselves derived from various other official sources, including the quarterly *Housing Statistics, Great Britain*, the *Monthly Bulletin of Construction Statistics* (both published by the Department of the Environment), and the

Housing Return for Scotland (Scottish Development Department). A useful summary reference for statistics relating to housing conditions, output and finance, is the annual *Social Trends,* material for which is drawn mainly from the sources referred to above. The Department of the Environment also publishes a regular series of reports on housing conditions under the rubric of the *Housing Survey Report Series,* and numerous reports on the construction industry have been prepared by the Department's building research unit.

At the international level, summary data on housing output and housing amenities are published in the United Nations *Statistical Yearbook.* This includes estimates for each country of the number of dwellings and/or the number of buildings, and floor area, completed for habitation each year. With respect to housing stock and amenities, the *Yearbook* includes estimates of the number of households, number of dwellings, average size of household, average size of dwellings, percentage of owner-occupied dwellings, percentage of dwellings with water, sanitation and other amenities, and derived statistics of housing densities. As with other UN data, these statistics are based on returns from member countries, and the availability and quality of these statistics are highly variable.

For European countries, more detailed information is available from the United Nations *Annual Bulletin of Housing and Building Statistics for Europe.* For each country, estimates (supplied by participating countries) are published of annual increases, decreases, and hence net changes in the stock of dwellings. Interestingly, the figures for Ireland include an estimate for depletions based on an annual rate of 0.7 per cent of the total stock, referred to in section 4.2. In addition, the UN *Bulletin* includes an analysis of new dwellings completed by number of rooms, percentage of new dwellings completed with various facilities, including central heating, and a classification of new dwellings by type of dwelling. Some of the data published for Ireland in this volume are not available in the *Quarterly Bulletin* or in any other domestic published source.

SOURCES AND REFERENCES

OFFICIAL SOURCES

(a) Ireland

Census of Population 1961, Vol. VI, CSO (Dublin: Stationery
    Office)
Census of Population 1966, Vol. VI, CSO (Dublin: Stationery
    Office)
Census of Population 1971, Vol. VI and Vol. VII, CSO (Dublin:
    Stationery Office)
Irish Statistical Bulletin, CSO (Dublin: Stationery Office)
National Income and Expenditure, annual, CSO (Dublin:
    Stationery Office)
Quarterly Bulletin of Housing Statistics, Department of Local
    Government (Dublin: Stationery Office)
Report of the Department of Local Government, annual
    (Dublin: Stationery Office)
Returns of Local Taxation, annual, Department of Local
    Government (Dublin: Stationery Office)
Statistical Abstract of Ireland, annual, CSO (Dublin: Stationery
    Office)

(a) UK and International

See Section 4.4. Additional references:
Abstract of Regional Statistics, annual, CSO (London: HMSO)
A Statistical Survey of the Housing Situation in European
    Countries around 1960, Geneva, UN Economic Commission
    for Europe, 1965

OTHER REFERENCES
    [1] Department of Local Government, Housing in Ireland,
         1969 (Dublin: Stationery Office)
    [2] H.B. Early, 'Construction Industry Statistics', An Foras
         Forbartha, 1973
    [3] An Foras Forbartha, 'Report on New House Prices', 1972

[4] P.R. Kaim-Caudle, 'Housing in Ireland: Some Economic Aspects', ESRI Paper No.28, 1965

[5] F. Kennedy, 'Public Expenditure in Ireland on Housing in the Post-War Period', *Economic and Social Review*, III, 3, 1972

[6] P.J. Meghen, *Housing in Ireland*, Dublin: Institute of Public Adminstration, 1965

[7] A.S. Muire, P.A.R. Hillyard, D.J.O. Roche, 'An Index of Housing Conditions for Ireland', *Social Studies* (Irish Journal of Sociology) I, 3, 1972

[8] T. O'Beirne, 'Family Size and Dwelling Size', An Foras Forbartha, 1971

[9] P. O h-Uiginn, 'Some Social and Economic Aspects of Housing: An International Comparison', *Journal of the Statistical and Social Inquiry Society of Ireland*, XX, 3, 1959-60 (also *Administration*, VIII, 1, 1960)

[10] *Housing – Progress and Prospects*, Pr. 7981, Dublin: Stationery Office, 1964

[11] *Housing in the Seventies*, Prl. 658, Dublin: Stationery Office, 1969

[12] Paul A. Pfretzschner, *The Dynamics of Irish Housing*, Dublin: Institute of Public Administration, 1965

CHAPTER 5

EDUCATION

EDUCATION, like health and housing, ranks as a major functional category in public authorities' expenditure on social services. The collection and publication of statistics of education serve a wide variety of purposes. Basic statistics of numbers of pupils, students and teachers, and derived measures such as pupil-teacher ratios and class-size distributions, are essential for assessments of the adequacy of educational services provided and for planning changes in the system. In conjunction with demographic data, current educational statistics provide a basis for forecasts of future demand for educational services, teacher requirements and physical facilities. The resources needed for the implementation of certain policy decisions or goals, such as raising the school-leaving age or achieving a lower pupil-teacher ratio, can be estimated. In the economy as a whole, second- and third-level education have assumed considerable importance in relation to forecasts of manpower requirements – e.g. assuming a certain rate of growth in national product over the next few years, what are the likely demands for certain categories of skilled labour, and can the educational sector satisfy these demands?

Statistics of the educational sector at any time correspond to the concept of a 'stock'; statistics for successive periods form a time series which enables analyses of the trends in stock to be made, and which approximate to measures of flow through the educational sector. Thus, starting with a particular cohort at age 6 years, we can in principle trace its progress through various levels of education up to university level. This approach provides the basis for 'models' of the educational sector and a systematic framework for quantitative analyses of educational systems and policies. Discussion of such models is beyond the scope of this chapter, but references [2] and [8] at the end of this chapter are recommended for further reading on this interesting topic.

Sections 5.1 to 5.3, which summarise published statistics of education in Ireland, are fairly brief. In the last ten years a number of special reports have added quite considerably to the amount of published data about education in Ireland, but regularly published data is sparse, particularly in comparison with Britain and with Northern Ireland.

5.1   PRIMARY, SECONDARY AND VOCATIONAL EDUCATION

Statistics relating to primary, secondary and vocational education are published by the Department of Education, through the publication *Tuarascáil — Táblái Staitistic*. Unfortunately, publication of this report is irregular and often several years out of date.

With respect to primary schools, the report includes statistics of the number of schools (of various types), the number of teachers, and the number of pupils enrolled; a classification of schools by average enrolment and number of teachers; a breakdown of pupils by age and class standard; an analysis of class-sizes, and the religious denomination of pupils. In some editions of the report, separate statistics are published for each county and county borough.

Other statistics published include numbers of trained and untrained men and women teachers in the service, distinguishing lay and religious teachers; numbers of teachers in training, and results of teacher training examinations. A breakdown of public expenditure on teacher training colleges and national schools is also included in the report.

For secondary and comprehensive schools, a similar range of statistics is provided, though there is more emphasis on subjects studied and examination results. Tables include a detailed breakdown of the number of candidates for, and results of, the Intermediate and Leaving Certificate examinations, by subject. There are separate data for boys and girls.

The third main section of the *Statistical Tables* is concerned with vocational education. Over 130 000 persons were registered for some form of vocational education in 1971-72, and the report records total enrolments for such courses, by various forms of classification. Separate figures are shown for whole-time continuation education, whole-time technical education, day release courses for apprentices and miscellaneous evening courses. There is no breakdown of students by subject or course followed, but numbers of candidates and passes in certificate examinations are published, by subject. There is also an analysis of whole-time and part-time teaching staff, by subject-area.

The report also includes a brief section on residential homes, and special schools (formerly known as reformatory and industrial schools), which records, *inter alia*, the number of children in attendance at such schools and the circumstances of their committal. (For additional material on these institutions, see the excellent — and highly critical — *Report on the Reformatory and Industrial Schools Systems, 1970*.) The most recent edition of the *Statistical Tables* contains an additional section on the school transport service.

Some of the data published in the *Statistical Tables* are reproduced, in whole or summary form, in the more readily accessible *Statistical Abstract*. Another regular source is the annual *List of Recognised Post-Primary Schools* issued by the Department of Education. The *List*, which covers all secondary and comprehensive schools, secondary sections of primary schools, and vocational schools which provide continuation education, records for each county and county borough a list of recognised schools, pupil enrolments, and whether the school is a day school, a boarding school, or mixed day and boarding.

Estimated participation rates, commonly used in educational studies, are sometimes published in the *Statistical Tables*. These rates are defined as the percentage of persons in any age-group who are receiving full-time education. They are frequently used in international and intertemporal comparisons of education levels, in estimates or projections of demand for higher education, in projections of supply and demand for skilled manpower, and similar purposes. Up to school-leaving age participation rates are high (ideally 100 per cent) and then tend to fall off sharply after the minimum school-leaving age, but there are notable variations between countries, developed countries generally showing higher participation rates at all ages.

Although not a regular series, a valuable reference which includes a substantial volume of educational statistics is the report entitled *Investment in Education* [2]. This comprehensive survey includes data obtained from a census of schools in 1963 and 1964, as well as forecasts of pupil enrolments and teacher requirements based on certain assumptions about population growth, pupil/teacher ratios and participation rates. Apart from its other merits, the report is a good example of the use of statistical material for descriptive and analytical purposes.

5.2 HIGHER EDUCATION

Higher education statistics, based on returns submitted to the CSO by the universities, are published in the *Statistical Abstract*. These include an analysis of annual admissions to universities, by age and sex, a breakdown of students enrolled, by faculty, an analysis of degrees conferred by type of degree (honours, ordinary or higher degree) and faculty, and some statistics of academic staff employed. Separate figures are recorded for St Patrick's College, Maynooth, and some financial statistics are also published.

In recent years a number of special reports and other publications have appeared which contain additional data on higher education. The most important of these is the *Report* of the Commission on Higher Education [1] which included a considerable volume of statistics on universities and other institutions of higher education in Ireland, statistical comparisons with other countries, and estimates of future demand for various forms of higher education. In addition, various reports of the Higher Education Authority (HEA) have included statistics relating to various aspects of higher education.

One of the objectives of the HEA is to establish a comprehensive data base of higher education statistics, and this can be expected to yield a regular and much-needed flow of statistics on university and other third-level education. Discussion of the purpose and form of such a data base is summarised in the 1974 Progress Report of the HEA [7] which in addition includes statistics of student numbers and other data for the universities, the eight Regional Technical Colleges, and other third-level educational institutions.

5.3 THE 1966 AND 1971 CENSUSES

An especially valuable addition to educational statistics in recent years was the special survey on education which formed part of the 1966 census of population. This was the first time such an inquiry had been undertaken as part of the population census, and results of the inquiry were published as a separate volume in the census report (Vol. VII, 1970).

In terms of information sought, the aims of the inquiry were simple. These were to ascertain, for persons whose full-time education had ceased, the age at which full-time education had ended and the type of school, college or other educational establishment attended (despite this deliberate limitation of the scope of the inquiry, it appears that nearly five per cent of the replies were blank, incomplete or inconsistent with other data).

The introduction to the 1966 census report contains a useful commentary on the results, with summary tables. The main body of the report consists of tables which classify the population according to age at which full-time education ceased and/or highest type of educational establishment attended, and various demographic, social and economic variables such as present age, area of residence, occupation, industrial group and marital status. Separate tabulations are presented for males and females.

These data provide a rich source of information about the educational experience of the population and of variations in educational attainment between different groups in the population. For example, comparison of different age cohorts shows how the level and pattern of educational achievement have changed through time. Comparison of different occupational or industrial groups is useful in analysis of skill requirements in different occupations or industries, and in turn such data may provide the basis for estimates of future manpower requirements. In conjunction with other demographic and educational statistics, the census data can be used to estimate future requirements for educational facilities, on varying assumptions about future population and participation rates.

Further inquiries on educational attainments were included in the 1971 census, covering age at which full-time education ended, second- and third-level education experience, and scientific or technological qualifications held. Results of this survey will be published in future volumes of the census reports: some preliminary results have been published in nos. 40 and 41 of the series of preliminary bulletins issued on the census results.

5.4 UK AND INTERNATIONAL SOURCES

In many countries, education has been amongst the earliest of the state's interests in the general field of social services, comparable to the state's interest in foreign trade in the economic field. Partly for this reason, there is a comparatively generous provision of education statistics at international level, though, as usual, the quality varies noticeably between countries.

The most important sources are the publications of United Nations agencies, particuarly UNESCO. For basic comparisons and trends, the most useful source will be found to be the UNESCO annual *Statistical Yearbook*; this contains, *inter alia*, statistics of numbers of schools, pupils and teachers and pupil-teacher ratios for most countries, participation rates, average number of years schooling for different age and sex cohorts, higher education statistics and estimated literacy rates. Another quite useful regular series is the *International Yearbook of Education* published by UNESCO and the International Bureau of Education (Geneva). This contains summary statistics for each country of the number of pupils and teachers in first-, second- and third-level education; in addition the *Yearbook* contains brief country reports for each of the member countries, though these reports are of little value for serious research purposes.

There are a large number of special UNESCO publications which deal with particular aspects of education, for all countries, for particular groups of countries (e.g. South-East Asia, developing countries) and for individual countries. As a basic international reference, the most important of these (though by now a little out-dated) is the five-volume *World Survey of Education,* the first of which was published in 1955 and the last volume in 1971. In particular, Volume 2 (1958) concentrated on primary education, Volume 3 (1961) on secondary education, and Volume 4 (1966) on higher education.

The United Nations *Demographic Yearbook* for 1963 contains a number of tables of educational statistics — literacy and illiteracy rates for adult age cohorts, by sex, number of years of education completed, and numbers and percentage attending school in the age range 5-24.

Within the United Kingdom, historical differences in educational structure and administration are reflected in the issue of separate sets of statistics for England and Wales, Northern Ireland and Scotland. The annual *Statistics of Education* is published in six volumes, mainly relating to England and Wales; these include a comprehensive range of statistics on schools (primary and secondary), examination candidates, results, and school-leavers, further education (vocational and non-vocational), the training and supply of teachers, financial statistics, and universities (covering the whole UK). For Scotland, a similar though less comprehensive range of statistics is published in the annual *Scottish Educational Statistics* from data supplied by the Scottish Education Department. For Northern Ireland, two volumes of educational statistics are issued each year under the rubric of *Northern Ireland Education Statistics*, in content and coverage similar to Scotland. The range of data, and the style and regularity of presentation of UK educational statistics, show that Ireland lags badly behind in the quantity and quality of published data. This is particularly the case with education statistics, though it also applies generally to most social statistics.

Statistics for the UK as a whole, based principally upon the sources listed above, are published in the annual *Educational Statistics for the UK*. These include basic statistics of pupil enrolments, numbers of schools and numbers of teachers at different educational levels; participation rates, size analyses of schools and classes and pupil-teacher ratios; qualifications and destination of secondary school-leavers, and details of flows and output at higher education levels (technical colleges, universities, teacher training colleges).

Summary statistics derived from these sources also appear in a number of annual publications, including *Social Trends,* the *Annual Abstract of Statistics*, the Northern Ireland *Digest of Statistics* and the *Scottish Abstract of Statistics*. There are in addition a large number of special reports and publications issued by the Department of Education and Science and the Scottish Education Department. Information about current publications is available in the quarterly *Statistical News.*

SOURCES AND REFERENCES

OFFICIAL SOURCES

(a) Ireland

Census of Population 1966, Vol. VII, CSO (Dublin: Stationery Office)
Census of Population 1971, *Preliminary Bulletins* 40 and 41, CSO (Dublin: Stationery Office)
List of Recognised Post-Primary Schools, annual, Department of Education (Dublin: Stationery Office)
Statistical Abstract of Ireland, CSO (Dublin: Stationery Office)
Tuarascáil – Táblái Staitistic, Department of Education, (Dublin: Stationery Office)

(b) UK and International

See section 5.3. Additional references:
Higher Education, Report of the Commission on Higher Education, 1963 (London: HMSO)
International Handbook of Universities, International Association of Universities
World List: Universities and other Institutions of Higher Education, International Association of Universities

OTHER REFERENCES
[1] Commission on Higher Education *I – Presentation and Summary of Report,* 1967, and *II – Report,* Vols I and II, 1967, Dublin: Stationery Office
[2] Department of Education, *Investment in Education,* Report, Annexes and Appendices, 1966, Dublin: Stationery Office
[3] Department of Education, *Report on the Reformatory*

and Industrial Schools Systems, 1970, Dublin: Stationery Office

[4]   Higher Education Authority, *First Report 1968-69,* 1969, Dublin: Stationery Office

[5]   Higher Education Authority, *Report on University Reorganisation,* 1972, Dublin: Stationery Office

[6]   Higher Education Authority, *Report on the Ballymun Project,* 1972, Dublin: Stationery Office

[7]   Higher Education Authority, *Progress Report, 1974,* Dublin: Stationery Office

[8]   W.J. Hyland, 'Education and Irish Society – with special reference to education needs', *Journal of the Statistical and Social Inquiry Society of Ireland,* XXII, 3, 1970-71

[9]   T.J. McElligott, *Education in Ireland,* Dublin: Institute of Public Administration, 1966

[10]   M. Nevin, *School Performance and University Achievement,* Higher Education Authority, 1974, Dublin: Stationery Office

[11]   T. A. O Culleanain, 'Special Education in Ireland'. *Oideas,* Fomhar, 1968

[12]   M. O'Donoghue, *Economic Dimensions in Education,* Dublin: Gill & Macmillan 1971

[13]   J. Rudd, *National School Terminal Leavers,* Dublin: Germaine Publications 1972

[14]   Steering Committee on Technical Education, *Report to the Minister for Education on Regional Technical Colleges,* 1967, Dublin: Stationery Office

CHAPTER 6

SOCIAL SECURITY

THIS chapter is concerned with statistics arising from the operation of schemes of social insurance and social assistance administered by, and under the general direction of, the Department of Social Welfare. These welfare schemes are concerned with such important social phenomena as unemployment, poverty, old age, disability and with various forms of family support. Statistical information collected through the operation of these schemes is therefore of considerable importance.

The present system of social insurance and social assistance in Ireland has evolved over a long period of years, and continues to change year by year. A useful introductory guide to the services available is provided by the periodic *Summary of Social Insurance and Social Assistance Services* published for the Department of Social Welfare by the Stationery Office.

Social *insurance* involves the payment of regular contributions in exchange for the right to specified cash benefits in the event of unemployment, disability, old age, etc. Subject to certain exceptions, social insurance is compulsory for all persons employed under a contract of service or apprenticeship.[1] However, certain categories of employed persons are compulsorily insured for only a limited range of benefits. The largest group in the labour force excluded from compulsory insurance is the

1 Up to 1 April 1974 insurance was not provided for non-manual employees whose rate of remuneration exceeded £1600 p.a.

self-employed, who are particularly numerous in agriculture and distributive trades. Prior to recent changes extending the coverage of the scheme, it appears that roughly 70 per cent of the total labour force came within the scope of compulsory social insurance, though some are insured only for certain benefits. There is also a scheme of voluntary insurance, available to persons who paid a certain minimum number of contributions under the compulsory scheme, but who then ceased to come within its scope. The voluntary scheme covers a specified range of benefits.

The social insurance fund is financed by contributions from employers, employees and the state. Up to 1 April 1974 both contributions and benefits were 'flat-rate', i.e., what an insured person paid in contribution, or received in benefit, did not vary with earnings. However, for many employees contributions are now related to earnings, and likewise various benefits, including unemployment benefit, vary according to these pay-related contributions.[2]

Benefits currently available under the social insurance scheme include unemployment, disability, occupational injuries,[3] treatment, maternity and deserted wife's benefits; contributory old age, retirement, contributory widow's and invalidity pensions; contributory orphan's allowances and death grants.

Subject to various conditions, persons insured under the Social Welfare Act may also be entitled to redundancy payments, administered by the Department of Labour, and, with their dependants, may be entitled to various health services administered by the health boards.

Social *assistance* schemes are designed to provide help in cash or kind to persons not covered by social insurance, or whose benefits under social insurance may have expired, or who otherwise may be considered in need of supplementary assistance. Receipt of social assistance involves a means test, the nature of which depends on the particular assistance scheme. Benefits presently available under these schemes include unemployment assistance, non-contributory old age, widow's and orphan's pensions, blind person's pension, and

2   At the time of writing, graduated or pay-related contributions apply to rates of earnings up to £2500.

3   There is a separate insurance fund for occupational injuries. See 6.2.

allowances for deserted wives, unmarried mothers, elderly single women and prisoners' wives. In addition, there are miscellaneous other schemes either administered by, or under the general direction of, the Department of Social Welfare. These include children's allowances (which do not depend on insurance or the application of a means test), prescribed relative allowances, free electricity, fuel and travel, free or subsidised footwear, and home assistance.

Details of rates of contributions for social insurance, and benefit and assistance rates payable, are published in the *Summary of Social Insurance and Assistance Services,* and in the periodic *Reports* of the Department of Social Welfare. Information on individual services is also provided in separate leaflets issued by the Department.

It is not proposed in this chapter to catalogue the regulations, rates of contributions and benefits and numbers of beneficiaries involved in each of the various social insurance and assistance services. Individual schemes are adequately described in the various departmental publications mentioned. Instead, the purpose is to present a summary view of the type and scope of social welfare services provided within certain broad areas of social policy, and to comment on the sources and interpretation of some of the main statistical series.

The following section 6.1 discusses statistics of unemployment. Although expenditure on unemployment benefit and assistance is not the largest component in social welfare expenditure, there is a greater volume of published data on unemployment than on any other aspect of the social services, and interpretation of the published statistics merits discussion in some detail. Other social welfare statistics, discussed in section 6.2, are published in much less detail, and there is little attempt to present or analyse the available data in ways which would prove useful to the evaluation or development of the particular social services concerned. This partly reflects the fact that statistical analysis or modelling of these areas of the social system has so far received little attention, in contrast to the techniques developed to describe the economic system and, more recently, the educational and health sectors.

6.1   UNEMPLOYMENT

Statistics of claimants to unemployment benefit and applicants for unemployment assistance are published in considerable detail in a variety of official publications. The source of these statistics, which are compiled by the CSO, is the local offices of the Department of Social Welfare, at which claimants to benefits and assistance must register. Persons registered include claimants to unemployment benefit, applicants for unemployment assistance, and other persons who are not currently eligible for either type of benefit, but who nevertheless register as unemployed. These three groups comprise what is called the 'live register'.

Several series based on the analysis of the live register are published by the CSO. A *weekly* statement records numbers on the live register at local employment offices, with separate figures for men, boys, women and girls. Claimants for unemployment benefit are broken down into farmers, farmers' relatives assisting, persons aged 65 and over, and others, and a similar breakdown is used for applicants for unemployment assistance. (Farmers and assisting relatives appear on the register by virtue of the fact that many smallholders work for part of the year in other occupations, such as construction.)

A *monthly* statement issued by the CSO contains an industrial analysis of the live register for a given week in that month. This records numbers on the register according to the industry in which persons are normally employed; statistics for the preceding month, and for the same month in the preceding year, are also recorded, the purpose here being to help identify the sources of changes in the live register.

An occupational analysis of the live register is issued by the CSO at *quarterly* intervals. This records the number on the register in a certain week in each quarter, broken down by stated occupation, with separate figures for males and females.

Many of these statistics are reproduced in the *Irish Statistical Bulletin,* which in addition includes estimates of unemployment percentages, for the country as a whole, for particular areas of the country, and for particular industry groups. These unemployment percentages are based on the ratio of the number of currently insured persons on the live register to the estimated currently insured population. The latter is estimated from the number and distribution of insurance cards exchanged in the preceding twelve-month period.[4]

Unemployment statistics are also published in the *Irish Statistical Bulletin*'s *Economic Series*. These include a series of total numbers on the live register at the end of each month; numbers on the live register who are resident in cities, urban districts and towns; percentage of currently insured persons who are unemployed around the middle of each month; number of claimants to unemployment benefit at the end of each month; and the amount expended on unemployment benefit in a week at the end of each month. Each issue of the *Irish Statistical Bulletin* records monthly data for the preceding three to four years, and also includes a graph for each series. Inspection of the data and graphs may suggest the existence of seasonal fluctuations in a particular series, and/or may indicate an upwards or downwards trend in a series.

As a measure of the number and percentage of persons unemployed, live register statistics are subject to some important qualifications. Legislative and administrative regulations affect the number of persons who register at any time, and changes in these regulations affect the comparability of data over time. Certain groups of persons — mainly smallholders — are excluded from the live register, and until fairly recently the operation of employment period orders[5] excluded certain persons in rural areas from receipt of unemployment assistance for certain periods of the year. Other persons who may be unemployed, such as school-leavers, may not register because they are entitled to neither unemployment benefit nor assistance. Moreover, changes in the definition of the live register, particularly in 1966, have affected the continuity of the series. Thus a number of factors — some tending to result in an underestimate of unemployment, and others in an overestimate — affect the accuracy of the live register as a measure of true unemployment, and variations over time in the unemployment series must be interpreted with caution. For an analysis of live

---

4 Insurance cards are exchanged annually, in January for males and in July for females.

5 Employment period orders were suspended in 1967. Apart from a limited period in 1971, they have not been reintroduced.

register statistics and a comparison of these statistics with persons recorded as 'out of work' in the 1966 Census of Population (Vol. V), see Geary and Hughes [4].

The same qualifications apply to the derived measures of unemployment percentages. These percentages are based only on the insured population, not on the total labour force, and they exclude persons engaged in agriculture, fishing and private domestic service. For a more detailed discussion of the limitations of the live register as a measure of unemployment, see the December 1965 issue of the *Irish Statistical Bulletin*; the matter is discussed also in chapter 2 of *Irish Economic Statistics* [11] and in the annual *Statistical Abstract*.

Examination of any particular series of unemployment statistics reveals one very obvious feature, namely seasonal variations in unemployment, which reflect seasonal variations in economic activity. Agriculture, food processing, tourism and construction are examples of industries in which the level of activity, and hence employment, varies quite markedly at different periods of the year. For this reason alone one would expect month-to-month variation in unemployment. In general, seasonal unemployment in Ireland reaches a peak in January-February, and is at its lowest in August-September. In analysing unemployment series, it is usual to try to eliminate the effects of seasonal factors to reveal the underlying 'trend' in unemployment. A method for smoothing time series to remove seasonal factors is explained in chapter 9.

Seasonally corrected monthly unemployment percentages are published in the annual *Trend of Employment and Unemployment*. This publication includes a considerable volume of data on unemployment, and a good commentary. Of particular interest are an analysis of the employment experience of males on the live register at a particular time in the year, and an analysis of the duration of unemployment of persons on the register. These data are important in attempting to distinguish between 'frictional' unemployment — in which unemployment is temporary and of short duration — and 'structural' or hard-core unemployment, which raises more difficult problems of social and economic policy.[6]

6 See Walsh [14].

Many of the series referred to are published, at least in summary form, in the *Statistical Abstract*. The *Report* of the Department of Social Welfare, which is published at irregular intervals, contains a useful summary of social insurance and social assistance schemes, and a large number of statistical tables. With respect to unemployment, these include weekly average number of claimants for unemployment benefit and applicants for unemployment assistance each year, and the number of claims and applications current on the last Friday of each month. Sources of income for social welfare schemes, and disbursements on unemployment benefits and assistance, are also recorded.

Finally, a special supplementary insurance scheme (called 'wet-time' insurance) for manual workers employed in the building, civil engineering and painting trades, covers interruption of employment due to bad weather. Contributions in the form of supplementary insurance stamps are shared between employers and employees, and benefits (at an hourly rate) are paid out to compensate for loss of wages due to bad weather. Details of the number of workers covered by this insurance scheme are published in the *Trend of Employment and Unemployment*.

6.2 OTHER SOCIAL SECURITY STATISTICS

Published statistics arising from the operation of other social insurance and social assistance schemes are less detailed, and are mainly limited to basic statistics of expenditure on, and numbers of beneficiaries of, the various schemes. Unlike the treatment of unemployment statistics, little attempt is made to analyse these data so as to show their social, economic or demographic significance.

As a point of reference, table 6.1 includes statistics selected to give a rough indication of the relative importance of the different social security schemes in operation. The available statistics can be conveniently described under three headings.

First, there are statistics arising from schemes concerned with the elderly, of which the most important are the contributory and non-contributory pension schemes. As table 6.1 shows, in 1970-71 approximately 71 per cent of the number of old age pensions and nearly 60 per cent of the value of old age pensions came under social assistance, which is means-tested (in 1970-71 only about one-fifth of non-contributory pensioners received a pension at the full rate). In contrast pensions payable under social insurance are paid independent of means, though a number of pensioners receive less than the full rate because they have not fully satisfied conditions with respect to number of insurance contributions.

Table 6.1   **Selected social security statistics**

(a)   expenditure on social security schemes 1970-71 (£000)

Unemployment benefit	10 656	
Unemployment assistance		9 241
Old age (contributory) pension	13 921	
Retirement pension	365	
Old age (non-contributory) pension*		20 272
Disability benefit	16 486	
Invalidity pension	1 058	
Treatment benefit	927	
Injury benefit	542	
Disablement benefit	617	
Death benefit	27	
Other occupational injuries benefits	167	
Widow's (contributory) pension	12 055	
Orphan's (contributory) allowance	71	
Maternity benefits	561	
Marriage benefit†	108	
Children's allowances		16 368
Widow's and orphans's (non-contributory) pensions		3 422
Miscellaneous grants and allowances		1 876

* includes pensions for the blind
† discontinued from October 1973

(b)   numbers of beneficiaries of various schemes

Date

31.3.71	Old age (contrib.) pensions	46 549
”	Retirement pensions	3 518
”	Old age (non-contrib.) pensions	113 570
”	Invalidity pensions	11 619
”	Disablement pensions	1 861
”	Widow's (contrib.) pension	53 238
”	Widow's (non-contrib.) pension	16 898
”	Orphan's (contrib.) allowance	538
”	Orphan's (non-contrib.) pension	147
”	Children's allowances − no. of families claiming	341 990
”	Deserted wife's allowance	1 284
”	Old age (care) allowance	1 859
”	Home assistance − no. of persons assisted	30 730
Year to 31.3.71	Unemployment benefit − average weekly claimants	38 752
” ”	Unemployment assistance − average weekly applicants*	23 519
” ”	Disability benefit − no. who received benefit	177 240
” ”	Injury benefit − no. who received benefit	9 808
” ”	Maternity grants paid	40 139
” ”	Maternity allowances paid	8 371

* Excluding smallholders
Note: Individuals may be included as beneficiaries under two or more of the above headings.
Source: Department of Social Welfare, *Report 1967-71*

Retirement pensions were introduced in 1970 to provide pensions for insured persons who retire at age 65, subject to retirement and contribution conditions. On reaching the qualifying age for old age pension,[7] retirement pensioners may, if it is to their advantage, claim old age pension instead, though maximum rates of benefit are the same for the two schemes.

There are in addition a number of other benefits available to elderly people. Pensioners who are incapacitated and who are receiving full-time care from a 'prescribed relative' can obtain an allowance in addition to their basic pension, subject to various conditions. Other allowances for pensioners include free travel on public (road and rail) transport, and, for certain categories of pensioners, free electricity and radio/television licences.

Statistics relating to these services are published in the *Statistical Abstract* and the *Reports* of the Department of Social Welfare (for brevity, DSW *Reports*). The *Abstract* records annual expenditure on pensions and number of pensioners classified by sex, marital status and rate of pension. These data are also published in the DSW *Reports,* which include some additional statistics such as a breakdown of the number of non-contributory pensions by county and county borough.

The second group of schemes to be considered are those involving temporary or permanent disablement. For occupational injuries or illness, benefits are available through the occupational injuries insurance scheme, which is financially separate from the general social insurance scheme. Occupational insurance is compulsory for almost all persons for whom social insurance is compulsory, as well as for some other categories not covered by social insurance. The scheme is financed by employers' contributions. The main benefits available are injury benefit and disablement benefit. Briefly, the former is payable, at a weekly rate, to persons who are temporarily incapacitated for work because of injury at work or illness attributable to work (occupational disease). The maximum duration of payment of injury benefit is 26 weeks, after which a person may, if eligible, be entitled to disability benefit under the general social insurance scheme (see below). Disablement benefit is designed to compensate for an assessed degree of loss of mental or physical faculty (varying from 1 per cent to 100 per cent) and comes into operation after the payment of injury benefit

7   At the time of writing, the qualifying age for old age pension is 67 for both men and women. It is intended that this should be reduced to 65.

ceases, or from the fourth day after the accident or development of the disease if injury benefit is not payable. The rate of benefit depends upon the degree of disablement, and may be paid as a lump sum or as a weekly pension. Various supplements to disablement benefit are also available in prescribed circumstances. As already explained, a recipient who is still unfit for work after injury benefit ceases may be entitled to disability benefit. Alternatively, if he or she is not entitled to disability benefit but is permanently incapable of work as a result of the occupational injury or disease, an *unemployability* supplement may be paid, at the same rate as disability benefit. An *attendance* allowance may be paid to beneficiaries who are a hundred per cent disabled and in need of whole or part-time attendance. Allowances for hospital treatment and medical care may also be claimed. In the case of fatal injury or illness, a pension may be paid to a surviving dependant or dependants, and a grant for funeral expenses is payable.

For non-occupational injuries or diseases, benefits are provided through the general social insurance scheme, subject to certain conditions regarding contributions. Disability benefit is available to insured persons during periods of incapacity to work. An insured person who has been in receipt of disability benefit for a year, and who is likely to be permanently incapable of work, may receive an *invalidity* pension (at the same rate of payment) as an alternative. Provided contribution conditions are satisfied, there is no limit to the duration of payment of disability benefit. As table 6.1 shows, disability benefits and invalidity pensions account for a substantial share of social security expenditure.

Insured persons are also entitled to *treatment* benefit, which covers the whole or part of the cost of dental treatment and dentures, spectacles, contact lenses and hearing aids, again subject to prescribed contribution conditions. Finally, under the Health Act (1947), a cash allowance is payable by health authorities to persons suffering from infectious diseases (mainly tuberculosis), and under the Health Act (1953) a cash allowance is payable to certain categories of chronically disabled persons.

Statistics relating to this group of social security schemes are published in the *Statistical Abstract* and the DSW *Reports.* The *Abstract* records the number of beneficiaries and value of various payments from the occupational injuries scheme, and similar data with respect to disability benefits from the social insurance fund, and maintenance allowance for persons suffering from infectious diseases and chronically disabled persons paid by the health authorities. More detailed statistics, including details of claims for treatment benefit, are published in the DSW *Reports*, though these appear only at four or five year intervals. In general, published data on these schemes are fairly limited.

The third main group of schemes to be considered are those designed to provide various forms of support and allowances to families. Of these the most important is children's allowances, involving a cash payment for each qualified child under the age of sixteen. Children's allowances, as already pointed out, do not depend on insurance payments or means tests but are payable as of right in respect of each qualified child. The principal requirement for qualification is residence.

Benefits and allowances under the social insurance schemes include widow's pension and orphan's allowance, payable to widows or orphans of insured persons, maternity allowance, payable on the wife's insurance only, maternity grant, which is payable on the husband's and/or wife's insurance, and deserted wife's benefit, also payable on her own or her husband's insurance. Details of rates of benefit, qualification conditions, etc., are included in the *Summary of Social Insurance and Assistance Services.* There are corresponding social assistance schemes for widows, orphans and deserted wives not entitled to a pension or allowance under social insurance. These are means-tested and the maximum benefits are less than those available under social insurance. In addition, social assistance allowances for unmarried mothers, prisoners' wives and elderly single women have recently been introduced; allowances are subject to a residence qualification and a means test.

One further scheme which should be mentioned is *home assistance.* Home assistance is financed through rates and administered by health boards and local authorities, subject to the overall direction of the Department of Social Welfare. It is designed to aid a person who is unable ". . . by his own industry or other lawful means, to provide the necessaries of life for himself or his dependants" (*Summary of Social Insurance and*

Assistance Services). In effect home assistance (which includes assistance in cash and kind) is the last line of support for persons who are not eligible for assistance from social insurance or social assistance or who cannot sustain an acceptable standard of living on whatever payments they do receive under these schemes. The continued existence of home assistance, which has its roots in the poor laws, is an indication of the gap in the social insurance and assistance schemes in Ireland, since although home assistance could be claimed to be one of these welfare services, it is a recourse of last resort and uncertain reliability. There are no detailed regulations on entitlement to home assistance or standard scales of assistance, and as a welfare service it can be said to be philosophically different from the other schemes described here. There is an excellent critical study of home assistance by Ó Cinneide [12].

The *Statistical Abstract* and the DSW *Reports* are again the main statistical sources for this group of schemes, though the statistics published are not very detailed. The *Abstract* includes a regional (county) breakdown of persons in receipt of home assistance, and expresses the number of recipients per thousand population in each area. Estimates of numbers of persons in receipt of home assistance each month are also published in the *Irish Statistical Bulletin*'s *Economic Series.*

In recent years there have been substantial changes in social security services in Ireland, and further changes can be anticipated as EEC member countries move towards a common system of social security. There is also scope for improvement in the presentation and analysis of social security statistics. As currently published, these statistics give little indication of the scope and significance of various social services as they affect different groups of people — for instance what is the proportion of elderly people who receive neither social insurance nor social assistance? — and in general it is difficult to assess the adequacy and importance of the different services available.

6.3 UK SOCIAL SECURITY STATISTICS

The structure of social insurance in the UK is broadly similar to that of Ireland. The coverage of the scheme is greater — for example the self-employed are included — and a somewhat greater range of benefits is available. As well as the standard flat-rate contributions and benefits, earnings-related contributions are levied and benefits provided under conditions similar to those in Ireland.

Non-contributory national assistance and pension schemes in the UK, which corresponded to the functions of social assistance in Ireland, were replaced in 1966 by a scheme of supplementary benefits. These benefits are payable to persons not in full-time work whose resources fall short of certain minimum requirements (which vary with family circumstances) established by the Department of Health and Social Security. Beneficiaries include not only those excluded from benefits under the social insurance scheme but also recipients of social insurance benefits whose income falls short of the minimum requirements established.

In addition, family income supplement (FIS) is designed for families with one or more children where the head of the family is in full-time work but family income falls below estimated minimum requirements. It includes cash and other welfare benefits. Both FIS and supplementary benefit are means-tested. In practice, though not in concept or structure, this brings the UK social security system close to the idea of a negative income tax or tax credit scheme.

The best statistical source for the UK is *Social Security Statistics,* an annual publication of the Department of Health and Social Security (prior to 1972, these statistics were published as part of the Department's *Annual Report*). This publication includes several hundred tables, recording rates of contribution and benefit and numbers of beneficiaries of various schemes; in many cases data are analysed by age, sex, region, family circumstances and period of time in receipt of benefit. Many of the statistics are estimated from sample data, and are therefore subject to sampling errors.

Most of the data in *Social Security Statistics* refer to Great Britain, though there is one section on the UK. Statistics for Northern Ireland are published annually in the Northern Ireland *Digest of Statistics.* Separate figures for Scotland are also published in the *Scottish Abstract of Statistics* and for Wales in the *Digest of Welsh Statistics.* Some other sources are listed at the end of the chapter.

Comparative international data on social security are

published regularly by the Social Security Administration of the United States Department of Health, Education and Welfare, by the International Labour Office and by the Commission of the European Communities. Some recent publications are listed in the references. For a comparative survey of social security schemes in Western Europe, a useful source is Kaim-Caudle [10]; for a recent discussion of social expenditure and social accounts in the EEC, see Broderick [1].

SOURCES AND REFERENCES

OFFICIAL SOURCES

(a) Ireland

Census of Population 1966, Vol. V, CSO (Dublin: Stationery Office)
Industrial Analysis of the Live Register, monthly, CSO (Dublin: Stationery Office)
Irish Statistical Bulletin (Dublin: Stationery Office)
Occupational classification of the Live Register, quarterly, CSO (Dublin: Stationery Office)
Reports of the Department of Social Welfare, annual (Dublin: Stationery Office)
Statistical Abstract of Ireland (Dublin: Stationery Office)
Summary of Social Insurance and Assistance Services, Department of Social Welfare (Dublin: Stationery Office)
Trend of Employment and Unemployment, annual, CSO (Dublin: Stationery Office)
Weekly Statement of the Live Register, CSO (Dublin: Stationery Office)

(b) UK and International

Abstract of Regional Statistics, annual, CSO (London: HMSO)
Annual Abstract of Statistics, CSO (London: HMSO)
Annual Report of the Department of Health and Social Security (London: HMSO)

Digest of Statistics, annual, Northern Ireland Office (Belfast: HMSO)

Digest of Welsh Statistics, annual, Welsh Office (Cardiff: HMSO)

Health and Social Security Statistics, annual, Department of Health and Social Security (London: HMSO)

Scottish Abstract of Statistics, annual, Scottish Office (Edinburgh: HMSO)

Social Security Statistics, annual, Department of Health and Social Security (London: HMSO)

Social Trends, annual, CSO (London: HMSO)

International Labour Office, *The Cost of Social Security,* (Geneva: ILO) 1972

Social Accounts 1970-1973 (Statistical Office of the European Communities) 1975

OTHER REFERENCES

[1] J. B. Broderick, 'Social Expenditure and the Social Accounts of the European Economic Community', *Journal of the Statistical and Social Inquiry Society of Ireland,* XXIII, 2, 1974-75.

[2] J. Deeny, *The Irish Worker. A Demographic Study of the Labour Force in Ireland,* Dublin: Institute of Public Administration, 1971

[3] D. Farley, *Social Insurance and Social Assistance in Ireland,* Dublin: Institute of Public Administration, 1964

[4] R.C. Geary, and J.G. Hughes, 'Certain Aspects of Non-Agricultural Unemployment in Ireland' ESRI Paper No. 52, 1970

[5] P.R. Kaim-Caudle, 'Social Security — Ireland and Western Europe', ESRI Paper No.20, 1964

[6] P.R. Kaim-Caudle, *Social Policy in the Irish Republic,* London: Routledge and Kegan Paul, 1967

[7] P.R. Kaim-Caudle, 'Compensation for Occupational Injuries', *Administration,* XIV, 1, 1966

[8] P.R. Kaim-Caudle, 'The Future of Social Services in the Irish Republic', *Administration,* XV, 4, 1967

[9] P.R. Kaim-Caudle, 'The Senior Citizen in Irish Society', *Administration,* XVII, 2, 1969

[10] P.R. Kaim-Caudle, *Comparative Social Policy and Social Security – a Ten-Country Study,* London: Martin Robertson 1973

[11] J. McGilvray, *Irish Economic Statistics,* (chapter 2), Dublin: Institute of Public Administration, 1969

[12] S. Ó Cinneide, *A Law for the Poor – A Study of Home Assistance in Ireland,* Dublin: Institute of Public Administration, 1970

[13] *Social Studies,* I, 4, 1972 (whole issue devoted to report of Conference on Poverty)

[14] B.M. Walsh, 'The Structure of Unemployment in Ireland, 1954-1972', Economic and Social Research Institute, Paper No. 77, 1974

CHAPTER 7

INCOMES, EXPENDITURE AND THE STANDARD OF LIVING

WHILE statistics of income and expenditure are classed as economic statistics, their inclusion in a book on social statistics should require little justification. Many debates and analyses of 'social' issues — for example, in health, housing, education and social security — require knowledge of contemporary economic circumstances, particularly those related to the level and distribution of incomes and the level and pattern of consumer expenditure. Moreover, the distribution of resources within a community is itself a matter of considerable social and political significance. For both these reasons, knowledge of the sources of statistics on incomes, wealth and expenditure is important.

7.1 INCOMES AND WEALTH

Of all statistics relevant to studies of the 'standard of living' and related issues such as poverty, those concerned with the level and distribution of personal incomes are the most important. This section discusses the concepts and definitions involved in the measurement of personal incomes and the main sources of statistics on income and wealth. Statistics of income will be discussed first.

At the outset, four main sources of information may be distinguished. First, aggregate data on income are generated through the compilation of the annual national accounts. Secondly, data on wages and salaries are collected through regular surveys of earnings such as the census of industrial production and other inquiries. Thirdly, a great deal of information is collected by the Revenue Commissioners through income tax and surtax returns. Fourthly, there are data collected by special surveys such as the household budget inquiry. Each of these sources has a number of limitations (including those of statistical accuracy) and, even taken together, are deficient in many respects, particularly in terms of information about income distribution.[1]

The most comprehensive but least detailed statistics of income are those compiled for the national accounts and published in the annual *National Income and Expenditure*. A description of the structure of the national accounts is given in chapter 6 of McGilvray [9] and only the barest summary will be given here, in as far as this is necessary for discussion of personal income statistics.

National income can be simply defined as the sum of (annual) payments for productive services accruing to permanent residents of the country. The main constituents of national income are wages, salaries, incomes from self-employment, and corporate profits. It also includes the net inflow of wages, profits and other factor incomes from the rest of the world.

By definition, national income is equal to the net value of goods and services produced in the country (called net domestic product) plus net factor incomes from abroad. This is called *net national product at factor cost* = national income.

During the course of the year, a certain proportion of the country's capital equipment (buildings, plant and machinery) will be worn out and will need to be replaced. The estimated cost of this replacement, called *depreciation,* can be added on to net national product at factor cost to give *gross* national product at factor cost.

If the government imposes taxes on goods and services produced, the market value of these goods and services will be higher than their cost of production or factor cost. Conversely, if the government subsidises the cost of production of certain goods and services, market value will be less than factor cost.

---

1. For a more extensive discussion of sources of data on income distribution in Ireland, see the report of the National Economic and Social Council [10].

Thus, gross national product at factor cost *plus* taxes on expenditure *less* subsidies gives gross national product *at market prices.*
The relationship between these various national income concepts is summarised in table 7.1.

Table 7.1   **National income and related aggregates**

National income	x
Net national product at factor cost	x
Net factor income from the rest of the world	f
Provision for depreciation	d
Net domestic product at factor cost	x - f
Gross national product at factor cost	x + d
Gross domestic product at factor cost	x - f + d
Taxes on expenditure	g
Subsidies	s
Gross domestic product at market prices	x - f + d + g - s
Gross national product at market prices	x + d + g - s

Finally, it is necessary to define *transfer incomes.* In principle, the only incomes included in national income are those which represent payments for productive services. Other types of incomes, notably old age pensions, unemployment benefits and assistance and other forms of social security payments do not represent payments for productive services and are not included in national income. Such incomes are called transfer payments or transfer incomes and simply represent a redistribution of national income via the tax system.

We are now in a position to discuss briefly certain constituent items in the national accounts.

Domestic product (gross or net, and at factor cost or market prices) provides a measure of the total value of goods and services produced by the community. National product divided by total population provides a measure of average per capita income, and such measures are frequently used in comparative studies of standards of living, though there are serious problems involved in comparisons of this kind.[2] Changes through time in aggregate or per capita income are also used as indicators of changes in the standard of living, though again careful qualifications are required when using national income statistics for this purpose.

The largest constituent of national income is wages and salaries, though the exact share of labour services in national income cannot be estimated precisely because the incomes of the self-employed and unincorporated enterprises contain elements of labour remuneration and profits. What is available as *personal income* comprises national income *less* the trading and investment income of government *less* the undistributed profits of companies *plus* transfer incomes. (For a precise definition, the reader should consult one of the *National Income and Expenditure* series.)

Personal income as defined above is gross of taxes on personal incomes (income tax and surtax and contributions to social insurance). If these taxes are deducted from personal income, the residual can be defined as *personal disposable income* which is either spent on consumers' goods and services, or saved. The trends in disposable income and its two components are also of interest as indicators of the standard of living. The level and composition of personal expenditure on consumers' goods and services are discussed in the following section.

National accounts data indicate the trends in aggregate income and its major components. Information on the incomes of specific groups in the labour force — and hence some information on income distribution — is derived from a number of sources, of which the most important are the annual census of industrial production, the quarterly industrial production inquiry, the quarterly inquiry on earnings and hours worked in the building and construction industry, the Labour Court and the Agricultural Wages Board. Results of several of these

2. See for example J. Bhagwati, *The Economics of Underdeveloped Countries,* World University Library, London, 1966, Part 1, which discusses some of these problems of comparison. These include the question of the international exchange rates to be used in converting to a common basis of valuation, the treatment of differences in relative prices, and the existence in many less developed countries of a substantial non-monetary sector.

inquiries are published regularly in the *Irish Statistical Bulletin.* Statistics from these and other sources are drawn together by the CSO and published in the annual *Statistics of Wages, Earnings and Hours of Work,* which is consequently the most comprehensive source of data on earnings in different industries and occupations.

The statistics collected relate mainly (though not exclusively) to manual workers in transportable goods industries, utilities, building and construction, agriculture and transport. There are little or no data available about non-manual workers, including persons engaged in public administration, professions, commerce and many service industries, though periodic censuses of distribution contain statistics of earnings of persons employed in retail and wholesale trades.[3]

Within the range of industries and occupations covered by the regular inquiries mentioned, statistics of average hourly and weekly wage rates and hours of work, numbers engaged and average earnings are collected for different areas, different industries and occupations and different categories of workers, and separately for males and females. Data sometimes refer to statutory minimum or negotiated minimum wage rates and hours of work. In addition to these basic statistics, *Statistics of Wages, Earnings and Hours of Work* includes tables which show the distribution of earnings in different industries. Index numbers of wage rates, which measure the percentage change in wage rates over time, are also included in this publication and in greater industry detail for earnings in the results of the quarterly industrial production inquiry reported in each issue of the *Irish Statistical Bulletin.* Summary statistics of earnings and hours worked, derived from these various sources, are published in the annual *Statistical Abstract.*

The regular inquiries discussed above provide a detailed but incomplete record of the level and distribution of incomes, since they cover only part of the total labour force, and part of incomes received. The obvious additional source for statistics of income and income distribution is the Office of the Revenue Commissioners, but unfortunately the Revenue Commissioners

3. First results of the census of distribution for 1971 were published in 1975 (Prl 4709, Stationery Office, Dublin).

do not publish statistics which classify incomes by range of income. In principle, such information is available from tax returns, and is widely used in other countries in studies and measures of differences in income distribution.[4] The annual reports of the Revenue Commissioners do contain a classification of surtax payers by income range, but only a very small number of incomes are assessed for surtax and these statistics consequently provide very limited information on income distribution. The matter is further complicated in Ireland because almost no information is available on farmers' incomes.[5] There is therefore a noticeable gap in knowledge of the distribution of incomes in Ireland. Studies of the distributional effects of fiscal policy, of the changing structure of employment, of slower or faster rates of growth in national income, and of poverty itself, are necessarily constrained by this lack of data.

A further source of information on personal incomes and expenditure and the distribution of income is the periodic household budget inquiries (HBI) undertaken by the CSO, the most recent of which refers to 1973. The HBI comprises a very detailed record of the income and expenditure of nearly 8000 randomly selected households for selected periods in 1973. Principal interest in the results of the HBI lies in the details of consumer expenditure recorded — discussed in the following two sections — but the inquiry also provides a random cross-section of the level and distribution of incomes. For various sub-groups of households (differentiated by area, household composition, social class, and other characteristics) the HBI records average gross income, average direct taxation and, by subtraction, average disposable household income. Gross income is taken to include earned income, investment income, imputed income from dwellings, and various transfer payments. Of course, since the published statistics of income are sub-group averages, income variations within groups are not revealed;

4. An important statistical tool in measuring inequalities in income and wealth is the 'Lorenz curve'. See below and chapter 9.

5. Some information on farm incomes is available from the national farm survey conducted by the CSO through 1955-58, and the more recent farm management surveys conducted by An Foras Taluntais in 1966-69.

the tables simply show differences in average incomes between groups of households.

Unofficial estimates of the distribution of income by county have been made by the ESRI; for the most recent estimates see Ross [14]. Another ESRI paper by Hughes [5], which analyses the changing shares of different forms of incomes in national income, is also of interest.

While adequate data on income distribution in Ireland are not currently available, information on the level and distribution of personal wealth in Ireland can be derived from estate duty records maintained by the Revenue Commissioners, and estimates of the distribution of wealth using these data have been made recently by Lyons [7]. In simple terms, if we assume that estates assessed for duty in any period of time are a representative sample of all estates, then by appropriate grossing-up procedures, estimates can be made of total personal wealth and its distribution by size of estate. Since estates below a certain net capital value are not assessed for duty, techniques have to be employed to estimate the aggregate value of small estates, and other *ad hoc* adjustments may be necessary to account for undervaluation of estates, *inter vivos* gifts, and other deficiencies in the basic data. Nevertheless, estimates calculated in this way can be claimed to depict approximately the distribution of personal wealth. A summary table of Lyons's estimates, recording the percentage distribution of personal wealth by size of estate, is shown in table 7.2.

Casual inspection of the figures in table 7.2 demonstrates considerable inequality in the distribution of personal wealth in Ireland — for instance that over 70 per cent of personal wealth in Ireland is owned by less than 6 per cent of the adult population. A useful and commonly used device for illustrating differences in the distribution of wealth (and of income) is the Lorenz curve. The techniques for drawing Lorenz curves are explained in chapter 9; the interpretation of the Lorenz curve will be explained in the example below.

From any point on the horizontal scale, draw an ordinate to intersect the Lorenz curve; from that intersection point, drop a perpendicular to the vertical axis, as shown by dotted lines in figure 7.1. From this we infer that 50 per cent of persons own 11 per cent of total personal wealth in the UK. Conversely the

Table 7.2 **Percentage distribution of adult population and wealth in Ireland, 1966** [6]

Net Capital		Percentage of Persons aged 21 or over	Percentage of Net Capital
Nil		64.972	0.000
Exceeding	*Not Exceeding*		
Nil	£5,000	29.690	28.438
£5,000	£10,000	2.724	15.650
£10,000	£20,000	1.568	17.926
£20,000	£50,000	0.822	20.477
£50,000	£100,000	0.177	9.912
Exceeding £100,000		0.047	7.597
Total		100.000	100.000

Source: P.M. Lyons, 'The Distribution of Personal Wealth in Ireland', ch. VI. in J. Bristow and A.A. Tait (eds), *Ireland: Problems of a Developing Economy* (Dublin: Gill & Macmillan, 1972).

'other half' of the population own the remaining 89 per cent. If wealth were equally distributed, the Lorenz curve would be identical with the diagonal line in the diagram. The more unequal the distribution, the greater will be the area between the diagonal and the Lorenz curve. If we call the area of the triangle OAO' = 1, a measure of inequality can be calculated from the ratio

$$\frac{\text{Area between the diagonal and the Lorenz curve}}{\text{Area of triangle OAO'}}$$

The nearer the Lorenz curve is to the diagonal, the smaller will be this ratio. This measure is called the *Gini coefficient of concentration,* and it can be used to compare the distribution of wealth in different countries, or in the same country at different times. In Britain, for example, the Gini coefficient was 0.76

6. In this table the individual items may not add to the totals shown because of rounding.

in 1960 and 0.65 in 1969, so suggesting a shift towards a more equal distribution of wealth between these dates. Note that the Gini coefficient must lie between 0 (corresponding to complete equality of distribution) and 1 (complete inequality). Note also that the Gini coefficient is simply a statistical measure; the inference that a particular distribution is 'good' or 'bad' is a value judgement, or, to be more technical, requires the specification of a social welfare function. Other measures of the distribution of income and wealth have been suggested [15].

Figure 7.1 **Lorenz diagram of the distribution of personal wealth in the UK, 1969** [7]

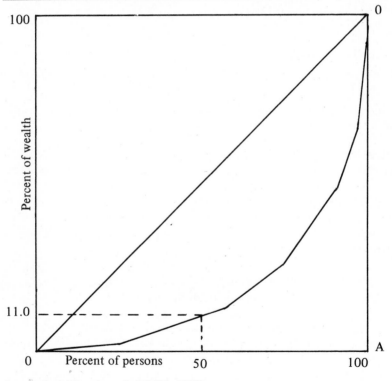

Source: *Social Trends,* no.2 (HMSO: 1971)

7. A Lorenz curve for the distribution of wealth in Ireland appears in Lyons, op.cit. This curve is not used here since the data are not entirely satisfactory for illustrative purposes.

Normally the distribution of wealth is more unequal than the distribution of income (either before or after direct taxes). This is to be expected *a priori* since differences in age and savings propensities would have the effect of creating differences in wealth, even if incomes were identical; differences in income, and inherited wealth, accentuate these differences.

7.2 CONSUMPTION AND THE STANDARD OF LIVING

Nowadays it is widely recognised that environmental factors such as pollution, density of population and recreational facilities should be considered in discussion of the standard of living. However, because it is very difficult to measure and ascribe values to these costs or benefits, the level of consumers' expenditure on goods and services is generally taken as the most important index of the standard of living. In an absolute sense, measures of individual or average consumption of goods and services have little significance. Given the prices of basic foodstuffs, it is possible to estimate the minimum level of expenditure required to satisfy a prescribed standard of nutrition (which would comprise a cheap but exceedingly monotonous diet). Similar calculations could be made for other necessities such as fuel, clothing and shelter, from which a subsistence level of consumption expenditure could be established. The income required to sustain this level of consumption would represent a 'break-even' level of income or 'poverty line'.

Although important — particularly in connexion with poverty in developing countries — the notion of subsistence levels of income and consumption is of little consequence to people's idea of the standard of living, which is viewed very largely in comparative terms. A 'high' or 'low' standard of living is assessed not so much in relation to a prescribed minimum standard, but in relation to the consumption levels of other individuals or communities. Individuals and communities habitually compare their consumption of goods and services with the consumption of other individuals and communities, or with their own consumption at an earlier time, and assess their standard of living accordingly. A level of per capita consumption which is said to reflect a high standard of living at one time may be regarded as a low standard of living several years later. Thus, in discussing the use of consumption statistics as indicators of the standard of living, we are primarily concerned with comparisons of consumption levels, between groups, between countries, and over time.

Since the standard of living is viewed in comparative terms, it may be inferred that little can be said about the standard of living on the basis of a single observation — for example, the level and distribution of consumption expenditure in Ireland in any one year. Fortunately, this is not entirely true. Economic research has demonstrated that as real incomes rise, the pattern of consumer expenditure changes in a particular way. A smaller proportion of income is spent on necessities such as food, clothing and fuel, while an increasing proportion is spent on consumer durable goods and services, such as education and leisure activities. Consequently, by examining the pattern of consumption expenditure at any moment, it is possible to make some judgements about the standard of living (though comparative concepts are still implicit in such judgements).

There are several sources of data on consumption expenditure in Ireland. Estimates of personal expenditure on consumers' goods and services are published annually in *National Income and Expenditure*. Tables show the estimated level and distribution of aggregate personal expenditure in the current year and earlier years, distinguishing up to fifteen different categories of expenditure. By way of illustration, table 7.3 reproduces personal expenditure estimates for 1960 and 1970.

Total personal expenditure rose by 126 per cent between 1960 and 1970 (though, since population rose slightly over this period, per capita personal expenditure rose by slightly less). However, since prices also rose over this period, it cannot be concluded that the standard of living improved by this proportion. Because prices in 1970 were generally higher, the actual increase in the quantity, or volume, of goods and services purchased was a good deal less than 126.0 per cent. The distinction between changes in value and changes in volume, and methods of separating the effects of each, are discussed in the following section.

Although the categories of expenditure used are fairly broad, certain trends in the pattern of expenditure are evident from these data. The most notable feature is the sharp fall in the proportion of expenditure on food. Signs of greater affluence

Table 7.3   **Expenditure of personal income at current market prices, 1960 and 1970**

Category	1970		1960	
	£m	%	£m	%
Food and non-alcoholic beverages	327.0	29.2	181.0	36.6
Clothing, footwear and personal equipment	125.0	11.2	52.0	10.5
Fuel and power (excl. motor spirit)	48.0	4.3	24.0	4.8
Alcoholic beverages	129.0	11.5	41.0	8.3
Tobacco	78.0	7.0	40.0	8.1
Durable household goods	59.0	5.3	21.0	4.2
Transport equipment	41.0	3.7	14.0	2.8
Other goods	80.0	7.1	29.0	5.9
Rent	68.0	6.1	30.0	6.1
Travelling within the State	68.0	6.1	27.0	5.5
Expenditure outside the State	42.0	3.8	15.0	3.0
Entertainment and sport	19.0	1.7	12.0	2.4
Professional services (inc. education)	39.0	3.5	16.0	3.2
Private domestic service	9.0	0.8	6.0	1.2
Other expenditure	65.0	5.8	28.0	5.7
Less expenditure by non-residents	-77.0	-6.9	-40.0	-8.1
Total: Personal expenditure on consumers' goods and services at current market prices	1120.0	100.0	495.0	100.0

Note: Figures here are rounded to the nearest £m, or first decimal, and may not add to total recorded, because of rounding. National accounts estimates are also subject to revision.
Source: *National Income and Expenditure 1970.*

are reflected in the higher shares of durable household goods, transport equipment, other goods, travel, and professional services in total expenditure. The increase in the share of alcoholic beverages owes less to the properties of alcohol as a 'luxury' good than to the sharp rise in excise duties on alcohol between 1960 and 1970.

This raises an important point of interpretation. Not only does the absolute price level vary, but relative prices of commodities and services vary through time, so that even if consumers bought the same quantities of goods and services each year, the proportions of expenditure would change. The figures in table 7.3 reflect changes in relative quantities and changes in relative prices.

Each category also includes expenditure by tourists and other non-residents. The actual allocation of expenditure by non-residents is not known precisely,[8] but an estimate for total non-resident expenditure is deducted to yield total personal expenditure by residents. Certain items of imputed expenditure or 'expenditure in kind' are also included, notably the imputed rental value of owner-occupied dwellings and consumption of own food produce by farm households.

Finally, while purchase of dwellings is not included with personal current expenditure, the purchase of other durable household goods such as furniture, cars, washing machines and the like are included. In practice, these goods yield a flow of consumption services over a period of years, and strictly speaking their purchase should be treated as investment, with an imputed value for their services distributed over the life-time of the asset. This is how housing is treated, with actual and imputed rental income representing the value of the consumption flow in each year. To follow this procedure for all durable household goods, however, would present formidable statistical and conceptual problems, and except for houses these goods are treated as totally consumed in the year in which they are first purchased. This means that during periods of household asset-formation, current consumption expenditure by households

8. However, detailed estimates of the level and composition of tourist expenditure in Ireland are compiled by Bord Failte, based on a variety of sources, including surveys of travellers, census of distribution data and other general and specific data.

will be overestimated, while for periods in which such assets are being run down, current consumption expenditure will be underestimated.

The household budget inquiry, mentioned in the previous section, is the most detailed source for analysis of consumers' expenditures. There are two important characteristics of the HBI survey data. First, they provide the most detailed breakdown available of household expenditure, distinguishing over three-hundred separate items of expenditure. Second, sample results are recorded separately for a variety of socio-economic categories, so that expenditure patterns for different groups of households can be compared. For example, one dimension of stratification is household size, thus enabling a comparison of the expenditure patterns of households of different size. Another important stratifying characteristic is gross weekly household income; as suggested above, the consumption pattern of households varies with income and the HBI data enable us to find out how. One of the motives to compare the consumption patterns of different income groups is to *predict* how consumption might change as income changes, a topic of considerable interest to economists. Studies of this kind are useful examples of *cross-section* analyses.

The inquiry is based on a sample and is thus liable to unavoidable sampling error as well as misreporting[9] and, prior to the 1973 survey, it covered only urban households. Moreover, it is conducted at fairly lengthy intervals, during which there may be significant changes in income, tastes and relative prices. Nevertheless the HBI is a valuable source of socio-economic data and is widely used as a source for applied economic research and market research.

It was suggested above that as incomes and the standard of living rise, the pattern of consumers' expenditure changes — the proportion of income devoted to 'necessities' falls and the proportion allocated to 'luxuries', such as consumer durables and travel, rises.[10] In addition to information contained in the

9. The HBI report notes an apparent understatement of incomes, while expenditure on alcohol is estimated to be understated by as much as 50 per cent.

10. Commodities and services for which demand rises more than proportionally as income increases are described by economists has having a 'high income elasticity of demand'.

national accounts and HBI, details of consumption of certain goods and services are available in other sources. These include data on stocks and/or flows of consumer durables such as motor vehicles, telephones, radio and television receivers, the level of hire purchase debt (used mainly to finance consumer durable expenditure) and expenditure on travel abroad. These items fall into the category of 'high income elastic' commodities and are therefore of particular interest as indicators of trends in the standard of living. For example, the ratio population/ number of currently registered private motor vehicles is commonly used in international comparisons as a comparative index of standard of living, on the assumption that possession of motor vehicles is closely correlated with income. Ratios such as population/TV receivers and population/telephone receivers are also used in this way.

Details of the number of private cars under current licence (the stock) and the number of new private cars registered and licensed for the first time (the gross flow, or addition to stock) are published in the *Statistical Abstract* (data for other types of mechanically-propelled road vehicles are also published). Data on licences current are disaggregated by county and county borough. New registrations are recorded for each calendar month, and this series is also published in the *Irish Statistical Bulletin* (Economic Series), while summary data are included in the *Reports* of the Department of Local Government. The *Statistical Abstract* also contains an analysis of new registrations by horse-power.[11]

Summary statistics of telephone and broadcasting services, derived from the records of the Department of Posts and Telegraphs, are published in the *Statistical Abstract*. These include the number of telephones available and the number of radio and television licences current. The distribution of radio and TV licences by county and the estimated number of licences per hundred population in each province are also published. Derived statistics such as the number of cars, telephones and television licences per hundred population are commonly used

---

11. A breakdown by horse power, by local authority area, and by unladen weight in the case of commercial vehicles, is also given in the 'Annual Vehicle Census', usually published each December by the Department of Local Government.

in inter-regional or international comparisons of living standards (though sceptics might question the contribution of these products to the quality of life). Nevertheless these measures are undoubtedly highly correlated with incomes, whatever their real contribution to living standards. Comparative data, showing car ownership, TV receivers and telephones per thousand inhabitants for some two dozen countries, including Ireland, are published in the *Administration Yearbook and Diary* [1]. This publication also contains other comparative indices related to living standards, such as GDP per capita and per capita daily intake of proteins.

Another indirect indicator of living standards — at least in consumer-oriented market economies — is the level of hire purchase debt, which in the household sector of the economy is used mainly to finance consumer-durable expenditure. Annual estimates of hire purchase and credit sales in Ireland, based on a survey of finance companies and trading concerns conducted by the CSO, are published regularly in the *Statistical Bulletin* and subsequently in the *Statistical Abstract*. Published data include the number of new agreements contracted each year, and the value of debt outstanding on all transactions at the end of the year. The number and value of new agreements are also classified by type of goods, including motor cars, radio and television sets, agricultural tractors and other agricultural equipment, furniture, apparel and drapery and other domestic electrical equipment. Except in the case of motor cars — by far the largest element in hire purchase debt — this classification provides an approximate distribution between hire purchase and credit sales to the business sector and to the household sector. The level and trend of (households') instalment debt outstanding is an indicator of households' acquisition of consumer-durable goods, in turn assumed to be correlated with the standard of living. In the same way as described for motor cars, telephones and television sets, the level of hire purchase debt outstanding per capita, or per household, can be looked on as an indirect indicator of comparative standards of living. However, even more so than for other measures, comparisons of hire purchase and credit transactions must be qualified by institutional and behavioural variations between countries, and within the same country over time.

Another element of consumers' expenditure which tends to grow rapidly with increasing affluence is holidays abroad, and expenditure on tourism abroad is therefore another indicator of standards of living. Estimates of the number of visits and of expenditure abroad by Irish residents are made each year by the CSO, using a sample inquiry called the passenger card inquiry,[12] and the results are published in the *Statistical Bulletin*. These statistics measure the number of visits outside the country, rather than the number of persons who travel abroad, and they include business as well as holiday travel, so the usefulness of the published data is limited by these qualifications. Nevertheless trends in these data are a further indication of changes in living standards.

Other important factors in considering the standard of living include the quality and availability of housing, health and education. Since these are the subject of separate chapters, they will not be discussed here, but ratios such as rooms per family, provision of housing amenities, number of doctors per thousand population, and participation rates in second- and third-level education are important and widely-used criteria in comparisons of living standards. Less obvious, but also important, are the effects of public expenditure on collective goods and services such as roads, parks, museums, public libraries and the like. It is misleading to view standards of living purely in terms of private expenditure on goods and services. Finally, assessment of a community's standard of living cannot be divorced from consideration of the distribution of resources within that community.

If a substantial proportion of the community live at below subsistence level it cannot be asserted that the *community* enjoys a high standard of living, even though many individuals within it may do so: any more than one could assert a community to be highly literate if 25 per cent of the people could not read or write. In summary, a wide variety of measures can be used to describe a community's comparative standard of living. The level of per capita income is the most commonly used, but no single measure can be used without careful

12. For a description of the passenger card inquiry, see the *Statistical Bulletin*, December 1959.

qualification, and the use of averages may conceal wide variations in living standards within the community.

7.3   PRICES AND THE COST OF LIVING

Changes in the standard of living depend not only on changes in money incomes but also on changes in the prices of goods and services which these incomes can buy. If an individual's disposable income (i.e. income after taxes and other deductions at source) rises by 10 per cent, while the prices of all goods and services rise by a uniform 15 per cent, then that individual will be worse off despite his higher money income. His 'real' income, as measured by the purchasing power of his money income, will have fallen. Particularly in periods of rapid inflation, it is important to distinguish between money incomes and incomes adjusted for price changes, the latter being commonly referred to as 'real' incomes or incomes at constant prices. In periods of inflation, it is not unusual for money incomes to rise while real incomes fall — which implies that prices are rising faster than money incomes. This distinction is important in studies of changes in the standard of living, in the distribution of income and wealth, and in international comparisons of standards of living; it is also important in wage negotiations.

At an aggregate level *National Income and Expenditure* contains estimates of national income or gross national product (GNP) in constant as well as in current prices. It is the constant price measure which records the 'real' change in the supply of goods and services from year to year, and which is therefore an appropriate concept for measuring changes in the standard of living. In periods of rising prices, GNP at current prices will increase more rapidly (decrease less rapidly) than GNP at constant prices. In times of falling prices GNP at current prices will rise more slowly (fall more rapidly) than GNP at constant prices.

Money incomes are observed data, while real incomes have to be estimated. Various methods of estimation are available but the basic procedure can be described in this way: the current money value of a particular aggregate (income, output, consumption, etc.) is *deflated* by means of a *price index* to yield an estimate of the value of that aggregate at constant prices. The resultant series represents real changes in the aggregate concerned.

A simple example may help. Suppose the current value of consumer expenditure rises from 100 in year one to 150 in year two, while prices uniformly double over the same period. A moment's reflection will suggest that real expenditure must have actually fallen over the period; arithmetically, dividing 150 (the current observed value of expenditure in year two) by 2.0 (the proportional change in prices) gives 75.0, which shows a fall of 25 per cent compared with year one expenditure. What we have done here is to deflate the value of expenditure in year two by a price index to yield an estimate of year two expenditure at the constant prices of year one.

It is not intended in this section to discuss in detail methods of deflation and their interpretation, but simply to indicate the distinction between real and money aggregates and the importance of price indices. From the foregoing it should be obvious that price indices are needed to distinguish between changes in the value of a particular aggregate and changes in its volume. The data in table 7.4, derived from *National Income and Expenditure* 1970, serve as an illustration.

Table 7.4 **Personal expenditure on consumers' goods and services at current market prices and constant (1958) market prices, 1958-65 (£m)**

	1958	1959	1960	1961	1962	1963	1964	1965
Expenditure at current market prices	459.2	465.8	495.3	522.1	562.5	600.4	668.9	704.7
Expenditure at constant (1958) market prices	459.2	463.9	488.9	504.0	522.6	544.0	568.3	573.2

Source: *National Income and Expenditure* 1970, tables B5 and B6.

The data in line one show the actual money value of

expenditure in each year. The data in line two have been estimated by deflating the data in line one by means of price indices. They represent the estimated value of expenditure at constant (1958) prices. Since the effects of price changes have been eliminated, the series in line two can be taken to show changes in the aggregate *volume* of expenditure from 1958 to 1965. Alternatively, we can view the data in line two as representing the physical quantities of goods and services consumed in each year, valued at 1958 prices. (If we had enough information on physical quantities, we could calculate the data in line two directly; deflating expenditure at current prices is an indirect method of achieving this result.)

Each series which is to be deflated requires a price index appropriate to that series: for example, an export price index, an import price index, an industrial production price index, and so on. This section will concentrate on one particular index considered to be of special interest, though the general principles discussed apply to all price index numbers.

The *consumer price index* is designed to measure changes through time in the overall (average) level of retail prices. Essentially this is achieved by comparing the current retail cost of a specified collection of goods and services with the same collection of goods and services at some fixed date in the past, called the 'base' period. The current cost is then expressed as a percentage of the base period cost, and this gives the value of the index for the current period.

This concept presents little difficulty in the case of a single commodity. Suppose a pint of beer costs 20 pence on 1 September 1972 and 24 pence on 1 September 1973. This represents a price change of +20 per cent. Let 1 September 1972 be the base period. Fixing the value of the index for the base period at 100, the value of this index for 1 September 1973 will be 120. If the price rises by a further 1 pence to 25 pence by 1 September 1974, then by similar reasoning the index for 1 September 1974 will be 125. In each period the cost is compared with the base period.

Even in this simple case, however, there are potential problems. The price of beer may vary between different retail outlets and a variety of values for the index can be obtained, depending on the retail outlet selected and whether the same retail outlet is used in each period. Secondly, the quality of the item may have changed between the two periods being compared — a possibility which increases, the greater the time interval between the current and base periods — and part of the price change may reflect this. For instance, the strength or gravity of the beer may have been increased (reduced), in which case it could be argued that an apparent increase of 20 per cent overstates (understates) the 'real' rise in price, which in principle should be based on the assumption of an unchanged homogeneous commodity. This problem of quality change affects almost all consumer goods, particularly consumer durable goods. Thirdly, unless price quotations are taken at the same time each year, seasonal variation in prices (especially in food prices) will influence the index and may give a misleading impression of trends in prices.

When the coverage of the index is extended to two or more items, further pitfalls emerge. Suppose the index is taken to include sausages as well as beer, and that the price of sausages falls from 30 pence per pound on 1 September 1972 to 28.5 pence on 1 September 1973. This represents a change of -5.0 per cent in the price of sausages, compared with a change of +20 per cent in the price of beer. To combine these, we could take the simple average of these changes, i.e., (+20%) + (-5%) ÷ 2 = 7.5%, and hence fix the value of the index at 107.5 for 1 September 1973. (1 September 1972 = 100).[13] But this would be incorrect, since it fails to reflect the fact that a given percentage change in the price of sausages has a greater impact on total outlay than an equal percentage change in the price of beer. To show this, the aggregate cost of a pint of beer and a pound of sausages in the base period is 20.0 + 30.0 = 50 pence, while the aggregate cost on 1 September 1973 is 24.0 + 28.5 = 52.5 pence. Expressing the latter as a percentage of base period cost, we obtain a value of 105.0 for the index (1 September 1972 = 100).

Extension of the index to more than two items poses no additional problems — the costs of all items are added together

---

13. This is equivalent to taking a simple average of the individual indices for the constituent items, i.e. price index for beer = 120, price index for sausages = 95.0, average = 107.5.

and the sum compared with the total cost of the same items in the base period. The exercise can be repeated for the next period, and so on, to generate a series.

A fundamental question, however, concerns the *weighting system* to be used in the construction of the index. Pursuing the example above, suppose the index were based on the changing cost of two pints of beer and one pound of sausages. Then the base period cost would be (2 x 20) + (1 x 30) = 70 pence and the 1 September 1973 cost would be (2 x 24) + (I x 28.5) = 76.5 pence. The index for September 1973 is therefore (76.5/70) x 100 = 109.3, which is different from the value of the index based on the cost of one pint of beer and one pound of sausages. From this, we deduce that unless all prices change in the same proportion, the value of the index will depend upon the relative quantities of the various commodities included in the basket of goods and services. The actual quantities used in the computation of the index are called 'weights', and the value of the index depends critically upon the relative weights chosen for the constituent items.

To be useful, the weights chosen for a consumer price index should reflect the average consumption pattern — the relative quantities of each item consumed — of the population, or of that section of the population to which the index refers. It should also be as comprehensive as possible in terms of the number of items included in the index.

The weights currently used in the official consumer price index described below are based on the household budget survey of 1973. From the sample data the proportional break-down of the expenditure of all households can be estimated, and these proportions form the basis of the weights used in the present consumer price index series. These weights replaced weights based on the 1965-66 household budget inquiry. Of course, the expenditure pattern of consumers changes, and the weights become increasingly unrepresentative of the actual pattern of consumer expenditure. This reduces the usefulness of the index, and so it is desirable to revise the weights from time to time. In 1974, the CSO introduced a small-scale continuing survey of households, to provide regular information on expenditure patterns and to indicate when it might be desirable to revise and update the index.

The consumer price index series is published in each issue of the *Irish Statistical Bulletin*. The base period for the index is now mid-November 1975 = 100, and is calculated at quarterly intervals (mid-November, mid-February, mid-May and mid-August). As well as an index for 'all items',[14] the CSO calculates and publishes indices for groups of items (food, clothing and footwear, etc). This is shown in table 7.5, which reproduces the values of the consumer price index series for each quarter of 1972 (when the base period for the index was mid-November 1968 = 100).

Figures in the last column show the value of the index for each quarter of 1972. Thus in mid-December 1972 the collection of goods and services comprising the index is estimated to have cost 39.2 per cent more than in the base period (mid-November 1968). Figures in the other columns of the table show the trend in costs of various sub-groups of items.

Since the CPI is computed on a quarterly basis, seasonal variations in certain prices will affect the index and may mask any underlying trend in prices. For this reason adjustments are made to the quoted prices for eggs, potatoes and tomatoes, to correct for seasonal variation, but undoubtedly other items are subject to seasonal variation and this should be remembered when analysing short-term movements in the index. Average annual values for the index are published in the economic series included in each issue of the *Statistical Bulletin*. These are averages of the four quarterly values.

For details of the construction of the index, and a lucid discussion of the problems and limitations, the reader is referred to the March 1976 issue of the *Statistical Bulletin* which contains an article introducing the current index series.

The consumer price index is not intended to represent a cost of living index, a concept which cannot be precisely defined in statistical terms. However it is frequently used as a proxy for changes in the cost of living, and within limits is a useful and valid reference for this kind of purpose. In conjunction with

14. The index is not universal in the sense that every possible item of consumer expenditure is included, but is designed to be comprehensive in the sense that almost every *type* of commodity or service is represented in the index. A small number of items are excluded because of practical difficulties of pricing, or on theoretical grounds. See the *ISB*, March 1976.

Table 7.5   Consumer Price Index: All items and commodity group index numbers (base period: mid-November 1968 = 100.0)

	Food	Alcoholic drink	Tobacco	Clothing & Footwear.	Fuel & Light	Housing	Durable household goods	Other goods	Transport	Services	All items
Mid-Feb. 1972	131.6	130.5	109.5	129.4	133.7	136.7	130.1	147.7	136.2	132.3	131.5
Mid-May 1972	134.6	130.8	109.6	131.8	134.0	137.7	132.2	149.8	137.7	135.4	133.5
Mid-Aug. 1972	140.9	131.2	109.7	135.2	140.6	143.2	134.8	151.3	139.1	137.7	137.2
Mid-Nov. 1972	141.4	134.1	109.4	139.6	142.9	148.2	138.7	152.7	141.4	140.1	139.2

Source: *Irish Statistical Bulletin*, December 1972

information about trends in disposable incomes, it can also be used to identify approximate trends in real incomes and the standard of living, as indicated at the beginning of this section.

7.4   UK AND INTERNATIONAL STATISTICS
There are numerous sources of UK statistics relating to incomes and earnings, wealth, consumers' expenditure and prices. Many of these are similar, in terms of primary sources and form of presentation, to the published sources for Ireland discussed in the preceding sections, but UK statistics are generally more extensive. As in Ireland, primary source material derives from (a) the compilation of national accounts data, (b) data collected by the Inland Revenue for taxation purposes and (c) regular surveys of incomes, earnings and prices, including the family expenditure survey, which is the UK equivalent of Ireland's household budget inquiry.

For aggregate data the most important source is the annual *National Income and Expenditure* (the *Blue Book*). Like the Irish equivalent, this includes estimates of total annual income accruing to UK residents and the main national income components such as wages and salaries, income from self-employment, income from investments and so on. Using data on aggregate taxes on income and social security benefits, national income can be adjusted to yield estimates of personal disposable incomes. The *Blue Book* is thus a basic source for analysis of the level and composition of national income and of trends in its major components (in aggregate or per capita terms). The main national accounts estimates are also published in the *Annual Abstract of Statistics,* while other useful sources are the *Monthly Digest of Statistics* and the monthly *Economic Trends* which include quarterly estimates of gross domestic product, disposable incomes and other national accounts data. For more detailed information on incomes there are three, or perhaps four, major primary sources − the annual *Inland Revenue Statistics*, compiled by the Board of Inland Revenue, the annual *Family Expenditure Survey*, the annual *New Earnings Survey* and the monthly Department of Employment *Gazette*, compiled by the Department of Employment.

The data published in *Inland Revenue Statistics* are derived from tax returns and are of particular interest with respect to income distribution. Published tables include analyses of the distribution of (the number of) incomes by income range, before and after taxation of incomes. Many of the detailed tables are based on a special annual sample of tax returns drawn from all returns submitted and the results of the sample survey are appropriately 'grossed up' to obtain estimates for all incomes — the results are thus subject to sampling error as well as errors and biases of one kind or another in the basic data.

The *Family Expenditure Survey* (FES) is broadly similar in design and intent to the household budget inquiry described in earlier sections of this chapter. The FES, however, is conducted annually and this increases its usefulness as a source of information on income and expenditure. The sample of households is proportionately much smaller than the HBI (in recent years, an average of about 7000 households have been included in the FES); sampling errors are accordingly greater and there is evidence that higher income households are markedly under-represented [3].

The published results of the FES are similar in form to the HBI; average income and expenditure data (the latter in great detail) are recorded for defined groups of households. Criteria for classification include income range, household composition and region. Useful data on the ownership of consumer durables are also published. The FES sample includes Northern Ireland, for which separate details are shown.

A daunting volume of statistics on earnings and hours worked are collected by the Department of Employment, the main published outlets being the *New Earnings Survey* (*NES*) and the monthly *Gazette* published by the Department. A variety of regular surveys are collected by the Department, of which the *NES* is the most important by virtue of its coverage of almost all sectors of the economy and occupations. It comprises an annual random sample of all employed persons.[15] Data are collected on earnings and hours worked, and the results analysed by region, industry, occupation, age, sex and various other criteria. The result is a highly detailed profile of relative earnings in different occupational and industrial groups,

15. For details see any issue of the *NES*. In 1973 some 172 000 persons were included in the sample.

supplementing the more compact aggregate data on income distribution recorded in *Inland Revenue Statistics*. Results of other surveys of earnings, as well as preliminary and summary *NES* data, are published regularly in the Department of Employment *Gazette*. Selected data and summary statistics from the four sources discussed above appear in various other publications, including the *Annual Abstract*, the *Monthly Digest* and the annual *Social Trends*.

Estimates of personal wealth and its distribution, using the general methods of estimation described in section 7.1, are made by the Inland Revenue and published in *Inland Revenue Statistics*. Gini coefficients of concentration are also calculated and published, providing a simple means of analysing trends in the distribution of wealth. For summary data on wealth (and income) distribution, an excellent source is *Social Trends*.

For details of the level and composition of consumers' expenditure, the main sources are the *Blue Book* and the *Family Expenditure Survey*. The former includes estimates of total consumers' expenditure and its composition by major categories of expenditure (food, drink, clothing, etc.), at current and constant market prices. The FES provides a much more detailed analysis of household expenditure, including analyses of expenditure patterns by different groups of households, though expenditure data are recorded at current year prices only. Useful summaries of national accounts and FES data are published in the *Annual Abstract* and in *Social Trends*. To distinguish between changes in money income and expenditure and changes in real income and expenditure, data on prices are required. Indices of retail prices for all items of consumers' expenditure, and for specific commodity groups, are calculated on a monthly basis by the Department of Employment and published in a number of sources, including the *Monthly Digest*. Prices of certain items are adjusted for seasonal variation, so that the reported monthly series gives some indication of underlying trends in the level of prices. Weights used in the compilation of the indices are adjusted periodically using information obtained from the FES. Together with data on earnings and taxation, these price indices can be used to estimate trends in real income and expenditure and the standard of living.

There is also a variety of sources for international data. For summary comparative statistics, useful references are the UN *Statistical Yearbook,* the UNESCO *Statistical Yearbook* and the UN *Yearbook of National Accounts Statistics.* The last-named is essentially a compendium of the national accounts statistics of member countries, using a standard form of national accounts to facilitate comparisons (the data are of highly variable quality). The other two yearbooks include, *inter alia,* estimates of the level of, and rate of growth in GNP per capita, consumer durable statistics such as private cars, TV receivers and telephones per hundred or thousand people, and comparative statistics on education, housing, health and similar indicators of living standards, some of which have been discussed in earlier chapters. On a less comprehensive scale, comparative data for different groups of countries are periodically published by international organisations such as the OECD (Organisation for Economic Cooperation and Development, comprising mainly developed countries) and the EEC (European Economic Community).

SOURCES AND REFERENCES

OFFICIAL SOURCES

(a) Ireland

Household Budget Inquiry 1965-66, CSO (Dublin: Stationery Office), 1969

Household Budget Survey 1973, CSO (Dublin: Stationery Office), 1976

Irish Statistical Bulletin (Dublin: Stationery Office)

National Income and Expenditure, annual, CSO (Dublin: Stationery Office)

Statistical Abstract of Ireland (Dublin: Stationery Office)

Statistics of Wages, Earnings and Hours of Work, annual, CSO (Dublin: Stationery Office)

Report of the Revenue Commissioners, annual (Dublin: Stationery Office)

(b) UK and International

Annual Abstract of Statistics (London: HMSO)
Department of Employment Gazette, monthly (London: HMSO)
Digest of Statistics, Northern Ireland Department of Finance (Belfast: HMSO)
Economic Trends, monthly, CSO (London: HMSO)
Family Expenditure Survey, annual, Department of Employment (London: HMSO)
Inland Revenue Statistics, annual, Board of Inland Revenue (London: HMSO)
Monthly Digest of Statistics, CSO (London: HMSO)
National Income and Expenditure, annual, CSO (London: HMSO)
New Earnings Survey, annual, Department of Employment (London: HMSO)
Social Trends, annual, CSO (London: HMSO)
UN Yearbook of National Accounts Statistics (New York: United Nations)
UN Statistical Yearbook (New York: United Nations)
UNESCO Statistical Yearbook (Paris: UNESCO)

OTHER REFERENCES

[1] *Administration Yearbook and Diary,* Dublin: Institute of Public Administration, annual 1967-
[2] A.B. Atkinson (ed.) *Wealth, Income and Inequality* Harmondsworth: Penguin, 1973
[3] C.V. Brown, *The Impact of Tax Changes on Income Distribution,* 1972 edition, London: Institute for Fiscal Studies, 1973
[4] T.A.B. Corley, 'The Personal Wealth of Northern Ireland 1920/60', *Journal of the Statistical and Social Inquiry Society of Ireland,* XXI, 1, 1962-63
[5] J.G. Hughes, 'The Functional Distribution of Income in Ireland 1938-70', Economic and Social Research Institute, Paper No. 65, 1972
[6] F. Kennedy, 'Public Social Expenditure in Ireland', Economic and Social Research Institute, Broadsheet No. 11, 1975

[7] P.M. Lyons, 'The Distribution of Personal Wealth in Ireland', ch. VI in J. Bristow and A.A. Tait (eds.), *Ireland: Problems of a Developing Economy*, Dublin: Gill and Macmillan, 1972

[8] P.M. Lyons, 'The Distribution of Personal Wealth in Ireland', *Economic and Social Review*, III, 2, 1972

[9] J. McGilvray, *Irish Economic Statistics*, Dublin: Institute of Public Administration, 1969

[10] National Economic and Social Council, 'Income Distribution: A Preliminary Report', Report No.11, 1975

[11] E. Nevin, 'The Ownership of Personal Property in Ireland', Economic and Social Research Institute, Paper No.1, 1961

[12] J. Pratschke, 'Income Expenditure Relations in Ireland 1965-66', Economic and Social Research Institute, Paper No.50, 1969

[13] L. Reason, 'Estimates of the Distribution of Non-Agricultural Incomes and Incidence of Certain Taxes', *Journal of the Statistical and Social Inquiry Society of Ireland*, XX, 4, 1960-61

[14] M. Ross, 'Further Data on County Incomes in the Sixties', Economic and Social Research Institute, Paper No.64, 1972

[15] A. Sen, *On Economic Inequality*, Oxford: Clarendon Press, 1975

[16] *Social Studies*, I, 4, 1972 (whole issue devoted to report of Conference on Poverty).

CHAPTER 8

OTHER SOCIAL STATISTICS

THE three sections of this chapter relate to quite separate areas, covering election statistics (8.1), statistics of crime (8.2) and of communications (8.3). The last two did not appear to merit separate chapters. Some readers may think that election statistics merit a separate chapter, and there is certainly enough material for such a chapter. However, primary sources of electoral statistics require little elaboration, and extensive discussion of electoral systems and analyses of electoral trends have been judged to fall outside the scope of this book. Section 8.1 is therefore confined to a brief description of the sources of electoral statistics.

References to UK and international sources are not included in this chapter. For the UK, the most appropriate general sources are *Social Trends* (HMSO, annual) and the *Annual Abstract of Statistics* (HMSO). For more specialised and detailed data, the best starting-point is the CSO's *List of Principal Statistical Series and Publications* (HMSO).

8.1 ELECTORAL STATISTICS
To vote in Dail elections, presidential elections and referenda, a voter must be a citizen aged eighteen or over and resident in Ireland.[1] Voters must also be listed on the electoral register, which is maintained by the county registrars. Residents who are

1. Defence forces serving with the UN abroad are entitled to a postal vote. Members of the defence forces and Garda Siochana within Ireland may also be eligible for a postal vote.

not Irish citizens are entitled to vote in local elections. Elections are conducted by means of the single transferable vote, in multi-member constituencies, which results in a system of proportional representation. (In local elections a person may be entitled to vote in more than one of the thirty-one local authority areas.)

The total numbers of Dail and local government electors on the register at particular dates are published in the *Statistical Abstract* for each county and county borough. The numbers of electors in each constituency are published in the Dail and local election returns compiled after each election by the Department of Local Government. In recent years the registered electorate has comprised about 58-59 per cent of the total population, the remainder being persons under twenty-one, other persons not entitled to vote, and persons eligible to vote but who had not registered. The registered proportion will now be higher as a result of the referendum of December 1972, which reduced the voting age to eighteen.[2] The electoral register is available for public inspection and in fact is widely used as a frame for sample surveys, particularly in market research (see chapter 10).

Of the sixty members of the Seanad only six (the university members) are directly elected. Eleven are nominated by the Taoiseach and forty-three are elected by an electoral college comprising local councillors, members of the new Dail and outgoing senators; in principle these members are supposed to represent various interests, such as agriculture, commerce, and so on.

Election statistics are published in a variety of sources. For Dail general elections, returns are collected and compiled by the Department of Local Government and published under the rubric of *Election Results and Transfer of Votes.* This contains full details of first preference votes, transfers and counts for each constituency; the names of candidates, elected members and party affiliation; results of by-elections to the previous Dail and certain other summary election statistics. The most recent issue also includes maps of the constituencies.

Details of constituency returns for the 1973 Dail and Seanad

2. The newly-enfranchised were unable to vote in the February 1973 Dail election, not having been eligible for the register in the previous October.

elections and presidential election, as well as summary results for previous elections and referenda, are published in Nealon's *Ireland: A Parliamentary Directory* [9] a valuable and comprehensive reference. This book also contains some analyses of the election results, a mass of information about deputies and senators, and details of the Northern Ireland Assembly elections and of Assembly members. Summary election statistics are also published in the *Administration Yearbook and Diary* and in even more summary form in the *Statistical Abstract*. Last, but not least, the newspapers generally provide election results and analyses within a day or so of polling.

Local election returns are also compiled by the Department of Local Government and, while results were hitherto unpublished, they were available in printed form from the Department; results of the 1974 local elections, however, were published in 1975. Summary statistics, including number of seats, number of electors, votes cast and percentage turnout are recorded for each county and county borough council as well as for urban district councils and town commissions. The number of candidates, percentage of first preference votes obtained and seats won by each party are also recorded.

Election statistics, like those of horse racing, provide considerable scope for analysis and speculation. These include calculations of 'swings' between parties (the percentage transfer of support from one party to another between elections), the effect of candidates' personalities on votes gained or lost, identification of the 'floating vote', marginal seats, and so on. The system of proportional representation and multi-member constituencies in Ireland makes statistical analysis of swings and other electoral phenomena more difficult than in Britain, whose electoral system is that of the single-member constituency and simple majority principle. Although swings can be calculated on the basis of first preference votes, these are not necessarily correlated very closely (if at all) with changes in party strength as measured by elected members. Overall, it is quite possible for one party to gain in terms of first preference votes and yet lose seats.

A good analysis of electoral behaviour in the 1969 and 1973 elections is contained in Knight and Baxter-Moore [6] in which a measure called the 'marginal seat ratio' is used to analyse changes in constituency voting between successive elections. Other useful references for analyses of recent election results include Nealon's *Directory* and Farrell [3]. Chubb [2], Hogan [5], McCracken [8], O'Leary [12] and Whyte [14] contain useful information on the principles and operation of proportional representation.

Turning from factual information on electoral behaviour, statistical studies of party affiliation and support are comparatively few. Results of sample surveys conducted by Gallup Poll in 1969 and Irish Marketing Surveys in 1970 were published in *Nusight* [10] and *This Week* [13] and a succinct description and analysis of these results are contained in Whyte [14]. The association between party support and such factors as socio-economic class, education, age, sex, home ownership and car ownership were examined. While many of these social and economic characteristics are correlated to some degree with support for a particular party, the party-social class link in Ireland appears to be less marked than in other European countries.

The use of sample surveys to elicit opinions on political, social and economic issues is an increasingly important aspect of applied research in the social sciences. Although, as explained in the introduction, many of these data are of a different nature to the statistics with which this book is mainly concerned, they should not be overlooked as a source of quantitative information. Elementary principles of sample survey methods are discussed in chapter 10.

8.2 JUSTICE

Problems of law and order are of increasing concern in contemporary society. Since crime and lesser legal infringements represent, to a greater or lesser degree, deviant social behaviour, their nature and extent are an important feature of contemporary social conditions. In Ireland, however, there has been comparatively little sociological work in this area.

There are three regular official sources of statistics arising from the administration of justice. These are the annual *Report on Crime* by the Commissioner of the Garda Síochána, the annual *Report on Prisons* and the annual *Statistical Abstract.*

The *Report on Crime* includes statistics of the number of

known indictable offences and number of prosecutions, by category of offence, as well as an analysis of persons convicted by age and sex. Data are broken down by area, and corresponding figures shown for preceding years. This enables trends in indictable offences to be identified, though it must be remembered that data relate only to offences known to the Garda and there may be variations through time − and from area to area − in the reporting of crime. Details of prosecutions for non-indictable offences, of which the large majority are for offences against the highway acts, are also reported. The statistics published in successive *Reports* provide a useful indication of trends (subject to the qualification noted) in the number and pattern of offences, and in detection rates for different types of offence.

The *Report on Prisons* contains a substantial volume of data on the prison population and certain aspects of prison conditions. These include the number of persons committed and discharged during the year, analysis of length of sentence and type of offence, ages of prisoners, and some information on prisoners with previous convictions (recidivists). The *Report* also includes statistics of cell occupancy rates, prison industries and offences committed during imprisonment.

Some of the data published in these reports are reproduced in whole or summary form in the *Statistical Abstract,* which also contains additional material provided by the Department of Justice. This is mainly concerned with the activities of the courts, and includes a breakdown by category of new cases before the courts, the results of court proceedings, and details of bankruptcy cases and offences against the liquor licensing laws. The preface to this section of the *Abstract* incidentally provides a brief description of the structure of the legal system.

Apart from these sources very little additional data is available, at least in published form. Noteworthy exceptions are the excellent *Report of the Commission of Inquiry on the Reformatory and Industrial Schools Systems,* and two studies of young offenders by Hart [17], [18]. Some additional references are listed at the end of this chapter, but they contain little statistical information.

8.3   COMMUNICATIONS

The term 'communications' is perhaps an imprecise description of the subject-matter of this section, which is taken to include statistics relating to newspapers and periodicals, television and radio, and advertising. These channels of communication are commonly referred to as 'the media'.

Official statistics relating to the media are sparse, though this is precisely one of the areas in which basic statistical information is of considerable interest to social scientists, and which should be integral to any range of statistics concerned with the social characteristics of a community. However, virtually no information on the media is published in the *Statistical Bulletin*, with the exception of a brief annual report on the activities of Irish advertising agencies. This report, which does not claim to be comprehensive, records advertising sales by medium (press, billposting, radio and television, film screen) and total employment, for those agencies included in the inquiry.[3] The report is generally published in the September or December issue of the *Bulletin*.

Some additional, though equally simple, statistics are published in the *Statistical Abstract*. As already mentioned in the previous chapter, the *Abstract* records the number and geographical distribution of radio and television licences current. It also includes an analysis of the output of sound and television broadcasting, by type of programme (music, news, sport, etc.); in the case of television there is a separate breakdown for home-produced and imported programmes. However, no information is given on the consumption of these services by listeners or viewers.

The other statistical series in the *Abstract* which is of some relevance is that related to municipal and county libraries. This series records for each county and county borough the number of library centres and (total) stock of books, though again no information is published on the utilisation of these facilities. These library statistics are also published in the *Reports* of the Department of Local Government.

For those interested in a more comprehensive view of the media in Ireland, a useful starting reference is the

---

3. Billings by non-Irish agencies are not included.

Communications   Directory   and   Yearbook compiled by O'Donnell and Fanning [23]. The *Directory* includes a list of newspapers and periodicals published and sold in Ireland; radio and television services; advertising, public relations, marketing and market research agencies; publishers and libraries. The statistical section of the *Directory* mainly comprises data drawn from other published sources, though it is useful to have them collected together. These include demographic statistics, business done by advertising agencies (derived from the *Statistical Bulletin*), advertising rates for newspapers and RTE and, more interestingly, some audience estimates for newspapers, periodicals, radio and television, and cinema. Summary breakdowns are given for sex, age, social class and region. These audience statistics are derived from the *Joint National Media Research Survey*, of which more below. In summary, the *Directory* is a useful source of reference on organisations and people involved in the communications industry, and for some background statistics on the 'media market'.

Within the particular area of broadcasting, RTE's *Annual Report* contains some statistical material, including an analysis of broadcasting hours by category of programme (reproduced in the *Statistical Abstract*), and a breakdown of advertising revenue by product type advertised. In addition, RTE, in conjunction with Irish Tam Limited and the advertising agencies, collects continuous information on programme viewing and, less frequently, conducts surveys of radio audiences. However, results of these surveys are not generally publicly available, though selected statistics are occasionally published in newspaper or RTE reports.

Undoubtedly the most comprehensive and interesting source of data in the area of communications in the *Joint National Media Research Survey*, sponsored by a consortium of newspaper proprietors and publishers, RTE, advertising and cinema interests, and conducted by Irish Marketing Surveys Limited. The results of this survey are not, of course, 'public statistics' in the sense of being freely available to users, but copies of the survey reports can be purchased and some results have been published in the newspapers.

In its present form the JNMR survey dates from 1972/73,[4] and is based on an annual sample of approximately 5 000 adult respondents. The sample is stratified by familiar demographic characteristics such as sex, age, socio-economic class, area, and marital status, but a wide range of less familiar economic and social characteristics are also used in the analysis — for instance, classifications of respondents according to household durables owned, whether smokers or non-smokers, and so on.

The primary object of the survey is to gather information about newspaper and periodical readership, cinema-going, radio listening and TV viewing, and the results are analysed in exhaustive detail, for the population as a whole and for numerous sub-groups within the population.[5] Although the function of the JNMR survey is to provide information for commercial advertising or marketing, the results provide in themselves an extremely interesting social and economic profile of the population, and provide virtually the only source of information on patterns of consumption of communications media. A brief description of the JNMR survey has been published in *Admap* [21].

4. Precursors were in 1968 (Gallup/British Market Research Bureau), 1969 (Market Research Bureau of Ireland) and 1970 (Market Research Bureau of Ireland).

5. Assuming the sample to be sufficiently 'representative', the sample results can be inferred to hold for the whole population. For further discussion of sampling, see chapter 10.

SELECTED REFERENCES

SECTION 8.1

OFFICIAL SOURCES

Election Results and Transfer of Votes, Department of Local Government (Dublin: Stationery Office)
Local Elections 1974: Results and Statistics, Department of Local Government
Statistical Abstract of Ireland, CSO (Dublin: Stationery Office)

OTHER REFERENCES
[1] *Administration Yearbook and Diary,* Dublin: Institute of Public Administration, annual
[2] Basil Chubb, *Cabinet Government in Ireland,* Dublin: Institute of Public Administration, 1974
[3] B. Farrell, 'Dail Deputies: The 1969 Generation', *Economic and Social Review,* II, 3, 1971
[4] G. FitzGerald, 'P.R. — The Great Debate',*Studies,* XLVIII, 1959
[5] J. Hogan, *Election and Representation,* Cork: Cork University Press, 1945
[6] J. Knight and N. Baxter-Moore, *Republic of Ireland: The General Elections of 1969 and 1973,* London: Arthur McDougall Fund, 1974
[7] M. Manning, *Irish Political Parties,* Dublin: Gill and Macmillan, 1972
[8] J.L. McCracken, *Representative Government in Ireland,* Oxford: Oxford University Press, 1958
[9] Ted Nealon, *Ireland: A Parliamentary Directory 1973-74,* Dublin: Institute of Public Administration, 1974
[10] *Nusight,* October 1969, December 1969, April 1970
[11] J.D. O'Donnell, *How Ireland is Governed,* (fifth edition), Dublin: Institute of Public Administration, 1974
[12] C. O'Leary, *The Irish Republic and Its Experiment with Proportional Representation,* Notre Dame, Indiana: University of Notre Dame Press, 1961
[13] *This Week,* 19 June, 1970
[14] J.H. Whyte, 'Ireland: Politics without Social Bases' in R. Rose (ed.), *Electoral Behaviour: A Comparative Handbook,* New York: Free Press, 1974
[15] Basil Chubb, *The Government and Politics of Ireland,* London: Oxford University Press, 1970

Parliamentary Directories for earlier years were compiled and edited by W.J. Flynn. For a list of these and other references not cited here, see the bibliography in Nealon's *Directory.*

SECTION 8.2

OFFICIAL SOURCES

Report on Crime by the Commissioner of the Garda Siochana, annual, (Dublin: Stationery Office)
Report on Prisons, Department of Justice (Dublin: Stationery Office)
Statistical Abstract of Ireland, CSO (Dublin: Stationery Office)

OTHER REFERENCES
[15] Rev. J. Byrne, 'Mountjoy Prison and the Irish Penal System', *Social Studies,* I, 3, June 1972
[16] Department of Education, *Report on the Reformatory and Industrial Schools Systems,* Dublin: Stationery Office, 1970
[17] Ian Hart, 'The Social and Psychological Characteristics of Institutionalised Young Offenders in Ireland', *Administration,* XVI, 2, 1967
[18] Ian Hart, 'A Survey of some Delinquent Boys in an Irish Industrial School and Reformatory', *Economic and Social Review,* I, 2, 1970
[19] Mary C. O'Flynn, 'Prison after-care in the Irish Republic', *The Irish Jurist,* VI, 1971
[20] N. Osborough, *Borstal in Ireland: Custodial Provision for the Young Adult Offender 1906-1974,* Dublin: Institute of Public Administration, 1975

SECTION 8.3

OFFICIAL SOURCES

Irish Statistical Bulletin, CSO (Dublin: Stationery Office)
Statistical Abstract, CSO (Dublin: Stationery Office)

OTHER REFERENCES
[21] *Admap,* April 1975 (Special report on Ireland)
[22] *Report of the Broadcasting Review Committee* 1974 Prl 3827, Dublin: Stationery Office

[23] J. O'Donnell and J. Fanning (eds.), *Communications Directory and Yearbook 1974/75*, Dublin: Mount Salus Press, 1975

[24] Radio Telefis Eireann, *Annual Report*

CHAPTER 9

SOME STATISTICAL CONCEPTS

PREVIOUS chapters have referred to various statistical terms, such as frequency distributions, time series and Lorenz curves. An understanding of these concepts is increasingly important for social scientists; as in other sciences, progress is marked by generalisation and conceptualisation in the form of quantitative models of behaviour. In this progression an understanding of statistical methods is imperative.

In this book reference to statistical method has been avoided as far as possible, but appreciation of some of the statistical sources discussed would certainly be enhanced if the reader had a basic understanding of a few simple statistical measures and techniques, and so this chapter on statistical concepts has been included. It explains the use of frequency distributions and summary descriptive measures such as the arithmetic mean; the basic concepts which underlie time series analysis, and the method of construction of Lorenz diagrams, which are referred to in chapter 7. It must be stressed, however, that what follows is not intended as a potted introduction to statistical methods. It is highly selective, concentrating only on statistical methods which are of relevance to the material discussed in chapters 1-7.

A second reason for its inclusion, specific to the material included in section 9.1, is to serve as a preliminary to the discussion of sample surveys in chapter 10. An understanding of frequency distributions and such measures as the arithmetic mean and standard deviation is essential to an understanding of sample survey methods.

9.1. DESCRIPTIVE MEASURES FOR FREQUENCY DISTRIBUTIONS
Consider the following (hypothetical) data concerning weekly
rent paid by a sample of 200 households.

Weekly rent (£):

0.90,	0.95,	1.00,	1.10,	1.24,	1.40,	1.50,	1.68,	1.70,
1.80,	1.87,	1.96,	2.00,	2.00,	2.00,	2.04,	2.10,	2.10,
2.17,	2.20,	2.25,	2.25,	2.30,	2.32,	2.38,	2.40,	2.44,
2.45,	2.50,	2.50,	2.50,	2.55,	2.60,	2.60,	2.62,	2.65,
2.70,	2.70,	2.70,	2.70,	2.75,	2.75,	2.80,	2.80,	2.82,
2.85,	2.90,	2.96,	2.98,	3.00,	3.00,	3.00,	3.00,	3.00,
3.05,	3.06,	3.10,	3.10,	3.12,	3.15,	3.15,	3.20,	3.20,
3.25,	3.25,	3.28,	3.30,	3.32,	3.35,	3.36,	3.36,	3.40,
3.40,	3.42,	3.45,	3.46,	3.48,	3.50,	3.50,	3.50,	3.50,
3.50,	3.60,	3.60,	3.60,	3.65,	3.70,	3.70,	3.70,	3.75,
3.75,	3.75,	3.76,	3.78,	3.80,	3.84,	3.85,	3.85,	3.87,
3.88,	3.90,	3.90,	3.90,	3.92,	3.95,	3.96,	3.98,	4.00,
4.00,	4.00,	4.04,	4.05,	4.10,	4.15,	4.15,	4.20,	4.22,
4.25,	4.25,	4.25,	4.30,	4.33,	4.35,	4.40,	4.40,	4.45,
4.50,	4.50,	4.50,	4.50,	4.55,	4.55,	4.60,	4.60,	4.62,
4.70,	4.75,	4.75.	4.80,	4.80,	4.80,	4.85,	4.88,	4.90,
4.90,	4.95,	4.95,	4.96,	5.00,	5.00,	5.00,	5.00,	5.00,
5.10,	5.10,	5.20,	5.25,	5.25,	5.40,	5.40,	5.50,	5.50,
5.55,	5.60,	5.65,	5.75,	5.75,	5.78,	5.80,	5.85,	5.92,
6.00,	6.10,	6.25,	6.25,	6.40,	6.50,	6.50,	6.50,	6.56,
6.56,	6.66,	6.75,	6.75,	6.80,	6.85,	7.00,	7.00,	7.50,
7.60,	8.00,	8.25,	8.80,	9.25,	9.75,	10.50,	11.75,	13.00,

14.50.

For convenience of exposition, the data have been arranged
in order of increasing value, though this is hardly the form in
which data are likely to arise in practice. Notwithstanding the
ordered arrangement, it is a very unwieldly mass of data. To
obtain a more concise picture, it is helpful to arrange the data
in the form of a *frequency distribution*, as shown in table 9.1.

This provides a good summary description of the distribution
of rents. The data have been grouped into *classes*. The difference
between the lowest value and the highest value in each class is
the *class interval*. Class intervals may be unequal; in this
example class intervals are equal except for the lowest class and
the two highest classes. The lowest and highest classes have not

been given specific class intervals.[1] Of course, given the raw data, classes and class intervals can be defined as we wish: the method of grouping the basic data is not unique, and depends on the judgement of the person organising the data and the purpose of the inquiry. The main point to bear in mind is that a frequency distribution is designed to present a concise but accurate description of the data.

Table 9.1 **Weekly rents of 200 households**

Weekly rent (£)	Number of households (frequency)
Less than 2.00	12
2.00 and under 3.00	37
3.00 ” ” 4.00	59
4.00 ” ” 5.00	41
5.00 ” ” 6.00	23
6.00 ” ” 7.00	15
7.00 ” ” 10.00	9
10.00 and over	4
	200

Two important rules should be followed in constructing frequency distributions. The classification must be *exhaustive* in the sense that any observation (value) can be allocated to a particular class. The classification must be *exclusive* in the sense that no observation can be allocated to more than one class. For example a classification of the form '2.00 to 3.00' and '3.00 to 4.00' is not exclusive since a value of 3.00 could be assigned to either class.

It will be noted that the frequency distribution involves a loss of information. The exact values of individual observations are not known when the data are given in this form.

1. Though of course we could do so by reference to the original data. However, for reasons which may become clearer later, it is useful to allow for the possibility of rents lower than the minimum or higher than the maximum of the rents included in the sample. On the other hand, for purposes of interpretation it is desirable to use equal class intervals in constructing frequency distributions.

In the example, the factor of interest is rent, and the data have been classified according to weekly rent. The factor of interest may be a *variable* or an *attribute*. A variable factor is one which assumes a numerical magnitude, like rent in the example. An attribute is a descriptive characteristic without a numerical dimension, like occupation, area or colour.

A variable may be *discrete* or *continuous*. A discrete variable is one which is defined to take only specific values along the continuum of real numbers. Thus 'rooms per dwelling' or 'children per family' are discrete variables since they can take integral (whole number) values only. Money is also a discrete variable, being defined in minimum units of a half penny.

A variable is continuous if for any two unequal values of the variable, however close together, another value can be found to fall between them. Thus weight is a continuous variable because unless two weights are equal, a third weight can be found (or defined) which falls between them.

In practice the distinction between continuous and discrete variables is less clear-cut. Money for instance is usually treated as a continuous variable since the interval between successive units is so small as to be insignificant for most purposes of analysis. And continuous units such as weight are in practice measured in discrete units determined by the precision of the measuring instruments used. Nevertheless, the distinction between continuous and discrete variables is important in statistics, though it will not be pursued here.

To return to our example, the frequency distribution summarises the salient features of the distribution. It is also possible to illustrate data in the form of bar charts, histograms and various other pictorial forms which are fully explained in any textbook on elementary statistics[2] and will not be discussed here. Instead, a number of important summary statistics will be defined, beginning with two important measures of central value.

Arithmetic Mean
This is the measure which in ordinary language is usually called

2. For example K.A. Yeomans, *Statistics for the Social Scientist: Introducing Statistics*, Harmondsworth: Penguin, 1968, ch. 2.

the average. To calculate the arithmetic mean, all the values are added together and their sum is divided by the number of observations. As with other measures of central value, the purpose of this measure is to describe the general level of magnitude of a set of values, by means of a single figure.

Adding together the 200 rents in our example, we obtain a grand total of £844.16. There are 200 observations, so that the arithmetic mean is $844.16 \div 200 = 4.2208$ or £4.22.

It is convenient here to introduce some simple notation. Let the variable of interest (in this case rent) be denoted by the letter x. In this example there are 200 values of x (rent) and to distinguish individual values a *subscript* is used. Thus the first observation is denoted by x_1, the second x_2, and so on up to x_{200}. Given the way in which the data are ordered, we have $x_1 = 0.90$, $x_2 = 0.95$, and so on up to $x_{200} = 14.50$. These are the values of the 200 observations on the variable x.

The sum of the values can be written $x_1 + x_2 + \ldots + x_{200}$. This is cumbersome, and the Greek capital letter Σ (sigma) is used to denote a summation, viz.

$$\Sigma x = x_1 + x_2 + x_3 + \ldots + x_{200}$$

so that Σx defines the sum of the values of the observations.[3]

The number of observations is usually denoted by N or n.

Finally, the arithmetic mean is commonly denoted by a letter with a bar over it; thus $\bar{x}$ denotes the mean value of the n observations of x.

We can now write the arithmetic mean rent in the following way

$$\bar{x} = \Sigma x \div n = 844.16 \div 200 = £4.22$$

At this stage an important property of the arithmetic mean should be noted. Suppose we subtract the arithmetic mean from each of the 200 individual observations. Thus $0.90 - 4.22 = -3.32$, $0.95 - 4.22 = -3.27$, and so on up to $14.50 - 4.22 = 10.28$. These are called *deviations* from (or about) the mean and are denoted by $x_1 - \bar{x}$, $x_2 - \bar{x}$, etc. Some of the deviations will be negative (observations below the mean) and

3. A more formal way of writing this is $\sum_{i=1}^{200} x_i$ which indicates that the sum is to be taken over 200 observations, starting at the first and continuing up to the 200th.

some will be positive (observations above the mean). However, the *sum of the deviations must equal zero*. Again, using our notation we can write this as

$$\Sigma(x - \bar{x}) = 0$$

Median

Although the arithmetic mean is the best known, it is by no means the only measure of central value. Amongst other measures available is the *median,* which can be defined as follows: If the observations are arranged in increasing order of magnitude, the median is the value of the middle observation. Thus if there are eleven observations, the median is the value of the sixth observation when they are arranged in order of magnitude. If there are an even number of observations, say twelve, the median is taken to be the value mid-way between the two middle observations, in this case between the sixth and seventh. In general the median is defined as the value of the $(n + 1)/2$th observation.

In our example there are 200 observations, so that the median observation is found as the $200 + 1/2 = 100.5$th, that is half-way between the 100th and the 101st when the observations are arranged in order of magnitude. From our original array of data (which are conveniently arranged in order of magnitude) the 100th observation is 3.87 and the 101st is 3.88, so that the value of the median is £3.875. (In practice we would probably take 3.87 or 3.88 as the median value, since from the original array it appears that figures are quoted to three significant places.)

The basic property of the median is that it divides the distribution into two halves − it is the middle observation, and in this respect can be treated as a representative or average value. Usually, the median and mean will take different values. The choice of the most appropriate measure to use in particular cases depends upon a number of considerations, for a discussion of which the reader should refer to a textbook on elementary statistics.

Both the mean and the median are descriptive measures which are designed to summarise a distribution by a single average or representative value. Before considering other measures, it will be explained how the mean and the median are calculated for grouped data, in the form of a frequency distribution like that of table 9.1.

The main point here is that the individual values of the observations are unknown, so that they cannot simply be added together to get a grand total. The simplest solution is to assume that each of the observations in a particular class can be represented by the mid-point of that class. For example in the class '2.00 and under 3.00' the mid-point can be taken as 2.50. There are 37 observations in this class, and it can be assumed that each of these can be represented by the value 2.50. Of course we know in fact that few of the observations actually take this value; however, if the 37 individual values are distributed approximately evenly in the range '2.00 and under 3.00', plus and minus deviations will tend to cancel out. In effect, we are taking 2.50 as the average value of the 37 observations in that class (going back to the original data, it will be found that the true mean of the 37 observations in this class is 2.496).

Table 9.2. sets out the data calculations.

Table 9.2

(1) Rent (£)		(2) Class mid-point (x)	(3) Frequency (f)	(4) fx	(5) Cumulated frequency
Less than 2.00		1.25	12	15.00	12
2.00 and under	3.00	2.50	37	92.50	49
3.00 "	" 4.00	3.50	59	206.50	108
4.00 "	" 5.00	4.50	41	184.50	149
5.00 "	" 6.00	5.50	23	126.50	172
6.00 "	" 7.00	6.50	15	97.50	187
7.00 "	" 10.00	8.50	9	76.50	196
10.00 and over		12.50	4	50.00	200
			200	849.00	

In column (2) the class mid-points are recorded. For the first and last classes, for which there are no defined class intervals, the class mid-points are arbitrary and judgement has to be exercised in specifying a representative value. This is an important point, since selection of an 'unrepresentative' value for these class mid-points could seriously distort the results. On the other hand it is often difficult to decide on a suitable representative value. For the lowest class, 1.25 has been taken as class mid-point instead of 1.00, on the grounds that there are unlikely to be many values below £1.00. For the highest class, £15.00 has been taken as the upper class limit and 12.50 as the class mid-point.

Column (3) records the frequency (number of observations). In column (4) the product of frequency times class mid-point is recorded, and the sum of this column (849.00) represents an estimate of total rent paid. It is of course only an estimate, which can be compared with the true figure of 844.16 − a very good approximation.

The arithmetic mean is now calculated as

$$\bar{x} = 849.00 \div 200 = 4.245 \text{ or } £4.25$$

To calculate the median for this frequency distribution, first note that the median observation was defined as the $(n + 1)/2$th observation. For reasons which will not be explained here, in the case of *grouped* data the median is defined as the $n/2$th observation. In our example this is $200/2 =$ the 100th observation.

It is now necessary to locate a particular value for the median observation. The median clearly does not fall into the first class, since there are only twelve observations with a value of less than £2.00. Adding the frequency in the first class to that in the second lowest, there are 49 observations with a value of less than £3.00 The median observation, which is the 100th has not yet been reached.

Adding now the frequency in the third lowest class (£3.00 and under £4.00) to the *cumulated* frequency of 49 for the first two classes, it is found that there are 108 observations with a value of less than £4.00. The median observation must therefore fall into the class £3.00 and under £4.00. (It is unnecessary to cumulate any further, but for the sake of completeness the cumulated frequencies up to the highest class are shown in column (5) of table 9.2).

A precise value for the median must now be specified,

somewhere in the interval £3.00 and under £4.00. This is found by assuming that the 59 observations in this class are uniformly distributed throughout the class and then 'counting along' until the median observation (the 100th) is reached. This process can be expressed formally in the expression

$$\text{Median} = 1 + \frac{\left(\frac{n}{2} - f_c\right)}{f_m} \times k$$

where

1 = lower class limit of the class in which the median is located

f_c = cumulated frequency up to the median class

f_m = frequency within the median class

k = the class interval

Applying this formula to the data in table 9.2 we get

$$\text{Median} = 3.00 + \frac{\frac{200}{2} - 49}{59} \times 1.00$$

$$= 3.00 + 51/59 \times 1.00$$
$$= 3.00 + 0.8644$$
$$= £3.8644 \text{ or } £3.86$$

This is the estimated value of the median for the grouped data, which can be compared with the 'true' median of £3.875 calculated from the ungrouped data.

Variance and Standard Deviation

The mean and median are designed to characterise a distribution in terms of an average or central value. Another important characteristic of a distribution is its 'spread' or 'dispersion'. For example, are the individual values closely grouped about the mean value, or are they widely scattered about the mean? There are several *measures of dispersion* of which the most important is the *variance* and its square root, the *standard deviation*.

It was explained above how deviations about the mean are calculated. The magnitude of these deviations gives some indication of how closely the individual values are grouped about the mean; the larger the deviations, the more dispersed are the observations about the mean. The average or mean of these deviations might therefore serve as an indication of the degree of dispersion — that is, add up the individual deviations, and divide by the total number (which is the same as the number of observations). Unfortunately this will not do since, as already noted, the *sum of deviations about the mean is zero.*

This difficulty is overcome by *squaring* each deviation — thus eliminating the minus signs — and adding together this sum of squares. In the case of our example of weekly rents, the first deviation was 0.90 - 4.22 = -3.32, which upon squaring becomes $(-3.32)^2 = 11.0224$; the second was 0.95 - 4.22 = -3.27, which upon squaring becomes $(-3.27)^2 = 10.6929$, and so on. All 200 squared deviations are then added together to give the sum of squares of the deviations, in our example 731.24. In terms of the notation introduced above, this sum can be written

$$\Sigma(x - \bar{x})^2 = 731.24$$

The sum of squared deviations is now divided by the of observations (n) to give what is called the *variance* example this is $731.24 \div 200 = £3.66$ or in notation $V(x) = \Sigma(x - \bar{x})^2 \div n$, where V(x) stands for the variance. (For reasons which need not be explained here, the denominator used is often (n - 1) rather than n.) The unit in which the variance is measured is the square of the original unit of measurement. For this reason the *square root* of the variance is commonly used as the measure of dispersion. This is called the *standard deviation.* Taking the square root of 3.66 gives 1.91, which is the standard deviation of the 200 rents in our example. This can be expressed as

$$s = \sqrt{\frac{\Sigma(x - \bar{x})^2}{n}}$$

(Because the standard deviation is written as s, the variance is often written as s^2.)

The variance and standard deviation are measures of the dispersion of values around their arithmetic mean. The larger the variance, the more dispersed or scattered are the observations about their central value. Other measures of dispersion are available, but variance is the most important.

To calculate the variance for grouped data, a process rather similar to that involved in the calculation of the arithmetic mean is used. Class mid-points are taken as representative of the values in each class, and deviations are weighted by the frequency in each class. The estimated variance for the frequency distribution of tables 9.1 and 9.2 is 4.02.

Though other descriptive measures are available, the measures described in this section are the most important and commonly used summary statistics for grouped and ungrouped data. The mean and variance are also very important in sampling theory, and their role in sampling will be discussed in the following chapter.

9.2 LORENZ CURVES

Lorenz curves were introduced in chapter 7 as a device for demonstrating the degree of inequality in the distribution of income or of wealth. In this section the method of construction of Lorenz curves will be explained, using as an example the distribution of agricultural holdings in Ireland.

The basic data showing the distribution of holdings by size of holding are shown in table 9.3.

The first two columns of the table represent a frequency distribution of the type described in section 9.1. In the third column the frequencies in the second column have been cumulated, by means explained in the previous section, when the calculation of the median was discussed. This tells us, for example, that 23095 holdings were of five acres or less; that 45993 holdings were ten acres or less, 67109 holdings were fifteen acres or less, and so on. As the reader may recall, the cumulated frequencies are obtained by adding together successive frequencies in the second column.

In the fourth column the data in the third column have been converted to percentages. Thus 8.26 per cent of all holdings are five acres or less, 16.46 per cent are ten acres or less, and so on. Each of the cumulated frequencies in the third column has been expressed as a percentage of the total number of holdings (279450). The data in this column represent one half of the information required for the construction of the Lorenz diagram.

Table 9.3   **Number of holdings classified by size of holding, Ireland 1970**

(1) Size of holding (acres)					(2) Number of holdings	(3) Cumulated frequency	(4) %Cumulated frequency
Above	1	and up to		5	23 095	23 095	8.26
"	5	"	"	" 10	22 898	45 993	16.46
"	10	"	"	" 15	21 116	67 109	24.01
"	15	"	"	" 30	65 773	132 882	47.55
"	30	"	"	" 50	60 235	193 117	69.12
"	50	"	"	" 100	56 238	249 355	89.22
"	100	"	"	" 150	16 864	266 219	95.27
"	150	"	"	" 200	6 487	272 706	97.59
"	200	"	"	" 300	4 242	276 948	99.10
Above	300				2 502	279 450	100.00
Total					279 450		

Source: *Statistical Abstract 1970-71*

The calculations required for the completion of the Lorenz curve are shown in table 9.4. The first column is identical to that in table 9.3. The second column shows the class mid-point for each class; for the last class, which is open-ended, we assume a class mid-point of 500 acres. The third column, which records the frequency in each class, is identical to the second column in table 9.3.

The fourth column of the table records the estimated total acreage accounted for by the number of holdings in each size category. If we assume that the average size of holding in the first class is three acres, and there are 23 095 holdings, then the total acreage accounted for by the holdings in this group is 3 x 23 095 = 69 285 acres. Similarly in the second class the class mid-point is 7.5 acres, there are 22 898 holdings and hence the estimated acreage is 7.5 x 22 898 = 171 735 acres. The remaining figures in the column are similarly calculated, as the product of the class mid-point and the corresponding frequency. Adding together the elements in the fourth column gives a grand total of 14 166 837.5 acres, which is the estimated acreage accounted for by all holdings in excess of one acre.

Table 9.4 Number of holdings classified by size of holding, Ireland 1970

(1) Size of holding (acres)	(2) Class mid-point (x)	(3) Frequency (f)	(4) fx	(5) Cumulated acreage	(6) % Cumulated frequency
Above 1 and up to 5	3.0	23 095	69 285.0	69 285.0	.49
" 5 " " 10	7.5	22 898	171 735.0	241 020.0	1.70
" 10 " " 15	12.5	21 116	263 950.0	504 970.0	3.56
" 15 " " 30	22.5	65 773	1 479 892.0	1 984 862.5	14.01
" 30 " " 50	40.0	60 235	2 409 400.0	4 394 262.5	31.02
" 50 " " 100	75.0	56 238	4 217 850.0	8 612 112.5	60.79
" 100 " " 150	125.0	16 864	2 108 000.0	10 720 112.5	75.67
" 150 " " 200	175.0	6 847	1 135 225.0	11 855 337.5	83.68
" 200 " " 300	250.0	4 242	1 060 500.0	12 915 837.5	91.17
Above 300	500.0	2 502	1 251 000.0	14 166 837.5	100.00
		279 450	14 166 837.5		

Source: *Statistical Abstract 1970-71*

In column five the acreage figures in column four have been cumulated. Thus holdings of five acres and under account for an estimated 69 285 acres, holdings of ten acres or less account for an estimated 241 020 acres, and so on. In the final column the data in column five have been expressed as cumulated percentage frequencies — thus holdings of five acres and under account for 0.49 per cent of the total estimated acreage, holdings of ten acres and under account for ·1.70 per cent of the total, and so on. Each figure in column five has been expressed as a percentage of the estimated total acreage (14 166 837.5).

We now have all the data necessary to construct the Lorenz diagram. However, to aid the discussion, the requisite data from tables 9.3 and 9.4 are shown together in table 9.5.

Table 9.5 **Cumulated percentage distribution of holdings and acreage by size of holding**

Size of holding (acres)	% of holdings	% of acreage
Above 1 and up to 5	8.26	.49
" " " " " 10	16.46	1.70
" " " " " 15	24.01	3.56
" " " " " 30	47.55	14.01
" " " " " 50	69.12	31.02
" " " " " 100	89.22	60.79
" " " " " 150	95.27	75.67
" " " " " 200	97.59	83.68
" " " " " 300	99.10	91.17
	100.00	100.00

From the first row of the table, those 8.26 per cent of total holdings which are five acres or less account for only 0.49 per cent of the total acreage. From the second row, the 16.46 per cent of holdings which are ten acres or less account for 1.70 per cent of total acreage. Subsequent rows are similarly interpreted. Reaching the second last row, it is observed that 99.10 per cent of holdings (i.e. all those of 300 acres or less) account for 91.17 per cent of total acreage. By subtraction, the top 0.90 per cent of holdings (i.e. those over 300 acres) account for 8.83 per cent of total acreage. Similarly, it can be calculated that slightly under 5 per cent of holdings (all those over 150 acres) account for nearly 25 per cent of the total acreage. In this way the table shows the extent of inequality in the distribution of agricultural land.

The Lorenz diagram illustrates the degree of inequality in diagrammatic form. Taking the bottom right triangle of the 'box' diagram in figure 9.1, the horizontal scale records the percentage of holdings, and the vertical axis records the percentage of total land area.

Figure 9.1 **Lorenz curve**

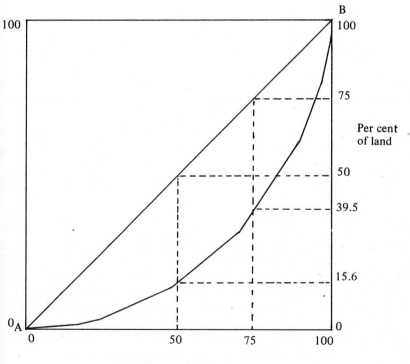

Per cent of holdings

The diagonal line joining points A and B has the important property that points on this line are equidistant from both the horizontal and vertical axes.

The Lorenz curve for the distribution is now drawn as follows. From table 9.5 we note that 8.26 per cent of holdings account for 0.49 per cent of total acreage. On the horizontal scale, mark the distance 8.26 and then, from that point, measure a distance 0.49 vertically. Mark this place with a dot or cross.

The next line of the table tells us that 16.46 per cent of the holdings account for 1.70 per cent of the land. Measure 16.46 along the horizontal axis, and then a distance of 1.70 vertically, to mark the next point.

The marking is repeated for each pair of values in table 9.5. When it has been completed, the points on the diagram are joined together by straight lines, which completes the drawing of the curve.

As explained in chapter 7, the further the curve lies from the diagonal line AB, the greater the degree of inequality in the distribution, illustrated in figure 9.1 by the dotted lines. For example, from the point 50 on the horizontal scale, the vertical distance between this point and the line AB is also 50, which would imply that 50 per cent of holdings accounted for 50 per cent of total acreage. A similar interpretation attaches to any other point on the diagonal − e.g. at 75.0 − so that the diagonal represents perfect equality in distribution. If all holdings were exactly the same size, the Lorenz curve would be the line AB, which is therefore known as the line of perfect equality.

In fact land is not equally distributed. For instance, the vertical distance between the point 50 on the horizontal scale and the actual Lorenz curve is approximately 15.6, which suggests[4] that the smallest 50 per cent of holdings account for only 15.6 per cent of total acreage − the 'top' 50 per cent of holdings therefore account for 84.4 per cent. Similarly the bottom 75 per cent of holdings account for an estimated 39.5 per cent of total acreage, leaving 60.5 per cent of total acreage in the possession of the top 25 per cent of holdings.

4. 'Suggests' because the curve can at best be regarded as an approximation of the actual distribution.

The example chosen here simply illustrates the methodology, and it is not intended to discuss the statistical qualifications relevant in this particular case,[5] or the broader questions of equity implicit in the use and construction of Lorenz curves. Although widely used, Lorenz curves have been strongly criticised as measures of inequality, and various alternative measures have been proposed and used.

9.3 TIME SERIES

Any set of observations on a variable, in which the observations are taken at different moments or intervals, comprises a *time series*. Observations are usually taken at regular intervals, such as monthly, quarterly or annually. The variables concerned may be *flows* or *stocks*; an example of the former is the volume of exports despatched in any period, and an example of the latter is the number of cattle noted at an agricultural census.

A substantial volume of data are collected on a regular basis by government departments and many of these are published as time series. A good example is the Economic Series published in each issue of the *Irish Statistical Bulletin* which in fact includes some series of social and demographic as well as purely economic statistics. Two of these series, and one other, are reproduced in table 9.6.

Even more than with frequency distributions, the use of charts and graphs is an invaluable aid to presentation and analysis of time series data. Figure 9.2 shows the data for the three series in table 9.6 in the form of time series charts or graphs. In all cases time is measured along the horizontal axis and the particular variable of interest along the vertical axis.

In table 9.6 (a) the data measure the monthly flow (output) of electricity. The horizontal scale in figure 9.2 (a) starts at the beginning of 1971 and, at equal intervals on this scale corresponding to one month, a distance is measured off on the vertical scale corresponding to the output for that month. The 'plot points' are then joined up by straight lines to form a continuous though irregular series.

---

5. These qualifications include the fact that agricultural holdings constitute only one element of personal wealth, the fact that the quality, and hence value, of land varies widely, and the fact that holdings of less than one acre are excluded.

Table 9.6   Time Series

(a) ESB generating stations: monthly output of electricity (million kWh)

Year	Jan.	Feb.	Mar.	Apr.	May	June	July	Aug.	Sept.	Oct.	Nov.	Dec.
1971	625.0	563.0	596.0	506.0	449.0	410.0	393.0	400.0	423.0	506.0	602.0	632.0
1972	687.0	633.0	634.0	460.0*	515.0	463.0	436.0	434.0	498.0	566.0	664.0	685.0
1973	716.0	653.0	670.0	609.0	585.0	480.0	496.0	482.0	529.0	646.0	635.0	735.0
1974	721.0											

* Output affected by shift workers' strike

Source: *Irish Statistical Bulletin* March 1974

(b) Total live register at the end of each month ('000)

Year	Jan.	Feb.	Mar.	Apr.	May	June	July	Aug.	Sept.	Oct.	Nov.	Dec.
1971	70.2	69.9	69.5	59.3	56.8	54.5	54.4	55.1	54.5	60.7	67.9	76.6
1972	79.0	78.2	77.4	75.1	70.8	68.5	67.2	68.5	66.4	67.9	70.2	74.8
1973	75.7	75.6	71.4	69.0	65.2	62.2	62.0	62.7	60.6	62.3	64.1	68.5
1974	72.4	72.3										

Note: Because of changes concerning eligibility for unemployment assistance, figures for April to October 1971 are not strictly comparable with those for other periods.

Source: *Irish Statistical Bulletin*, March 1974

(c) **Private motor cars registered and licensed for the first time 1963-70**

Year	Number	Year	Number
1963	37028	1967	40300
1964	41352	1968	51360
1965	43267	1969	50523
1966	39546	1970	52947

Source: *Statistical Abstract of Ireland* 1970-71

Table 9.6 (b) and figure 9:2 (b) show the number of persons on the live register at the end of each month. The time series graph has been constructed in a similar way to that of electricity output. Table 9.6 (c) and figure 9.2 (c) show the number of private motor cars registered and licensed for the first time, in each of the years 1963-1970. The data here are annual, but the principles of construction of the time series graph are the same. In all three cases the charts give a vivid picture of changes in the variables concerned over the respective time periods.

A wide range of techniques is available for analysing time series. These techniques derive from hypotheses about factors which may be held to influence the behaviour of a variable over time, though in any particular case not all, or even none, of these factors may play any role. The object of time series analysis is to identify, isolate and measure the influence (if any) of each of these factors in particular instances. Rather than continue in this abstract vein, a simple illustration of the general method of approach will be given, using the examples cited.

In the first two examples there is clearly a strong *seasonal* element present. Electricity output 'peaks' in the winter months (December to March) and 'troughs' in the summer months (June to August). The live register is similarly affected. Seasonality affects many economic and social time series, and is one of the general factors mentioned above. The presence of seasonality raises two questions for the analyst. First what are the nature and magnitude of the seasonal effect? Secondly, what would the time series look like with the seasonal influence removed?

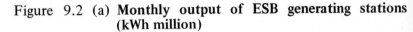

Figure 9.2 (a) **Monthly output of ESB generating stations (kWh million)**

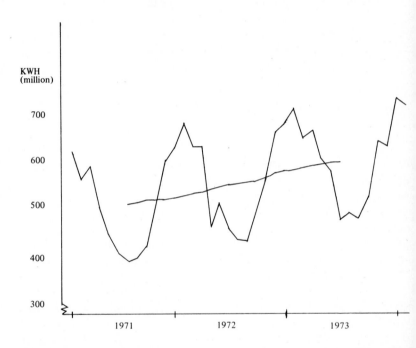

Before discussing these questions, note that in the third example the data do not permit the identification of any seasonal influence, since they are recorded on an annual basis. While new registrations may in fact vary seasonally, recording data on an annual basis eliminates seasonal fluctuations during the year. However, there is some slight evidence of *cyclical* fluctuations in new registrations. The number of new registrations does not demonstrate a regular movement in one direction but appears to peak and trough at intervals of roughly three years. Cyclical variation is another of the general factors which may influence a time series; the questions which the analyst attempts to answer with respect to cyclical variation, and the techniques employed, are similar to those used for analysing seasonal variations, to which we now return.

Figure 9.2 (b) **Total live register at the end of each month**

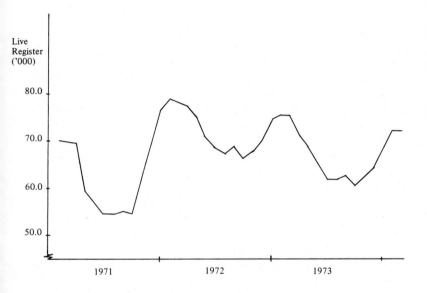

Figure 9.2 (c) **Private cars registered and licensed for the first time 1963-70**

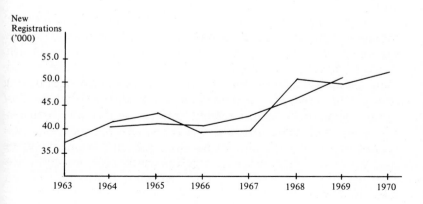

With respect to electricity output, it would be useful to identify and remove the seasonal component in the monthly figures, in an effort to identify the underlying *trend* — if any — in the data. The trend factor is the third factor considered as a potential influence on a time series, and it is usually the most important to identify. Two simple methods will be explained.

Suppose we take the twelve monthly figures for 1971 and calculate the monthly mean for that twelve-month period, which turns out to be 508.8 kwh. This figure is free of any seasonal component since it is an average for the year and evens out upwards and downwards variations in each month. Suppose now a similar calculation is carried out for the twelve-month period February 1971-January 1972, giving a mean value of 513.9. This figure is also free of any seasonal component, for the same reason, that it is an average for a continuous twelve-month period. Note that the average for the second twelve-month period is slightly higher. This is because output in January 1972 was higher than in January 1971 — output in each of the intervening months is common to both calculations.

The next step is to calculate the average output for the next twelve-month period, which is March 1971 to February 1972. And so on. At each step, the first observation in the series is replaced by the corresponding observation for the next year. If the pattern of seasonal effects is assumed to be constant from year to year, this procedure eliminates seasonal variation and ensures that the successive averages calculated are not influenced by variable seasonal effects, unlike the original series.

The averages calculated in this way are called 'moving averages' and are shown in table 9.7. The original data are shown in column two. Column three records twelve-month averages for the successive twelve-month periods. As noted above, average output for the first twelve-month period was 508.8. This average is recorded in the 'middle' of the twelve-month period to which it relates, in this case mid-way between the June and July outputs. Similarly for the next twelve-month period the middle lies between July and August, and so on. We continue computing twelve-month averages until we 'run out', the last period in this case being February 1973 to January 1974.

Table 9.7 **Electricity output: 12-month moving average**

(1) Month	(2) Output	(3) 12-month average	(4) 2-period average	(5) Ratio actual output ÷ moving average value
Jan 1971	625.0			
Feb "	563.0			
Mar "	596.0			
Apr "	506.0			
May "	449.0			
June "	410.0	508.8		
July "	393.0	513.9	511.4	.7685
Aug "	400.0	519.8	516.7	.7741
Sep "	423.0	522.9	521.4	.8113
Oct "	506.0	519.1	521.0	.9712
Nov "	602.0	524.6	521.9	1.1535
Dec "	632.0	529.0	526.8	1.1997
Jan 1972	687.0	532.6	530.8	1.2943
Feb "	633.0	535.4	534.0	1.1854
Mar "	634.0	541.7	538.6	1.1771
Apr "	460.0	546.7	544.2	.8453
May "	515.0	551.8	549.3	.9376
June "	463.0	556.3	554.1	.8356
July "	436.0	558.7	557.5	.7821
Aug "	434.0	560.3	559.5	.7757
Sep "	498.0	563.3	561.8	.8864
Oct "	566.0	575.8	569.6	.9937
Nov "	664.0	581.6	578.7	1.1474
Dec "	685.0	583.0	582.3	1.1764
Jan 1973	716.0	588.0	585.5	1.2229
Feb "	653.0	592.0	590.0	1.1068
Mar "	670.0	594.6	593.3	1.1293
Apr "	609.0	601.3	598.0	1.0184
May "	585.0	598.8	600.1	.9748
June "	480.0	603.0	600.9	.7988
July "	496.0	603.4	603.2	.8323
Aug "	482.0			
Sep "	529.0			
Oct "	646.0			
Nov "	635.0			
Dec "	735.0			
Jan 1974	721.0			

By construction, these averages eliminate seasonal variations and the resulting time series can be claimed to reflect the underlying trend in electricity output, though any cyclical component will still be reflected in these averages. For simplicity we shall assume that there is no cyclical component in electricity output (but see below).

As they stand, however, the moving averages are not directly comparable with the original series, since they are not 'centred' on calendar months but rather *between* calendar months. To get over this, we take two-period moving averages of the series in column three. For example, the mean of the first two figures in column three is $(508.8 + 513.9) \div 2 = 511.4$, and the 'middle' of these two observations is July 1971. Similarly, the average of the next two is $(513.9 + 519.8) \div 2 = 516.7$, and this is recorded opposite August 1971. It will be seen that the method of constructing the series in column four is exactly the same as that used for constructing the original series of moving averages, except that two-period averages are calculated instead of twelve-period averages.

The series in column four are the final moving average values. They have been plotted in figure 9.2 (a) along with the original series, and it will be seen how the moving averages 'smooth out' the series, and indicate the underlying trend. This is one of the objectives of the analysis.

Another objective may be to analyse the exact effect of seasonal variation. In column five of table 9.7, the recorded figures represent the ratios of the original values to the calculated moving average values. In July 1971, for example, the ratio is .7685 ($393.0 \div 511.4$). Actual electricity output in that month was .7685 or 76.85 per cent of the moving average value; if the latter is interpreted as the underlying 'trend' value, the ratio can be interpreted to mean that the seasonal effect in July reduced output by almost 24 per cent below its trend value. Similar effects are shown for July 1972 and July 1973, where actual output is 78.21 per cent and 82.23 per cent respectively of the moving average values.

For January, the seasonal effect works in the opposite direction. In January 1972 the actual output is 29.43 per cent above the moving average value, and for January 1973, 22.29 per cent above the moving average value.

The ratios for each month are reproduced in table 9.8. Except for April (the April 1972 figure was affected by a strike) the ratios for each month are roughly similar in magnitude. Although admittedly there are some wide variations in the values of the ratios for some months, it is possible even on the evidence of this very short series to gauge the general order of magnitude of the seasonal variation in each month. In practice such an analysis would be based on a much longer time series, but this simple example is sufficient to illustrate the general approach. Starting from the raw data, we have firstly attempted to identify any underlying trend in the series, and secondly attempted to measure the quantitative impact of the seasonal variation.

Table 9.8   **Ratios of actual to moving average values**

	1971	1972	1973
Jan		1.2943	1.2229
Feb		1.1854	1.1068
Mar		1.1771	1.1293
Apr		.8453	1.0184
May		.9376	.9748
June		.8356	.7988
July	.7685	.7821	.8223
Aug	.7741	.7757	
Sept	.8113	.8864	
Oct	.9712	.9937	
Nov	1.1535	1.1474	
Dec	1.1997	1.1764	

Although the use of moving averages is most common in the case of monthly or quarterly data, it can also be used with annual data, where there is known or suspected to be a cyclical component in the series. As a simple illustration, table 9.9 shows the calculation of three-year moving averages for the series on car registrations in table 9.6 (c). Here it is (rather riskily) assumed that there is a three-year cycle of boom-slump-recovery, superimposed on a gradually rising trend. A three-year moving average should therefore 'smooth out' the effects of cyclical variation and reveal the underlying trend, as in the case of seasonal variation. The data in table 9.9 and figure 9.2 (c) do lend some support to this hypothesis though in practice a much longer time series would be required before we could support such a hypothesis with any confidence. One problem with cyclical analysis, which does not arise with seasonal analysis, is that the length of the cycle may not be constant — business cycles, for example, may vary from three to five years.[6] When such variations occur, moving averages will not wholly remove cyclical influences and the moving average series could not be interpreted as trend values.

Table 9.9. **Private Car Registrations 1963-70**

Year	Number of registrations	3-year moving averages
1963	37028	
1964	91352	40549
1965	43267	41388
1966	39546	41038
1967	40300	43735
1968	51360	47394
1969	50523	51610
1970	52947	

One of the purposes in analysing time series, in addition to identifying seasonal, cyclical and trend components in the series, is to predict future values of the variable concerned. Although prediction by means of time series analysis is a hazardous as well as a not entirely respectable procedure, it is nevertheless widely used. Arguments about the circumstances in which time series is an appropriate forecasting device, and when it is not, will not be discussed here — the reader is simply warned to exercise considerable care in the use and interpretation of the technique.

6. Efforts to deal with seasonal variation also encounter problems. For example a particular series may not 'peak' or 'trough' in exactly the same period each year.

In simple terms, forecasting by means of time series analysis involves

(i)   identifying the trend component in the particular series;

(ii) describing the trend by means of an equation, in which the variable concerned is expressed as a function of time;

(iii) using the relationship obtained to estimate the value of the variable at any given future date — this is called the estimated trend value of the variable;

(iv) if required, the trend value can then be adjusted to include the seasonal and/or cyclical component.

Under (i), the use of moving averages to separate trend, seasonal and/or cyclical components has been explained. However, moving averages cannot be used to forecast — indeed, as the reader will have noticed, they do not even give us any values for the beginning and end of a series. An alternative is to describe the trend by drawing a freehand curve 'through the middle' of the plotted values, which will indicate the general trend in the series. In figure 9.3 this has been done for the series on electricity output, by simply fitting a ruler to the graph and drawing a line, shown by the dashed line on the graph. The reader will see that this line looks quite plausible as a description of the general trend in the series. To predict future values, the line is extended and the value of output read off the vertical scale (for February 1974 this gives a trend value of approximately 630.0 kwh). It should be noted that there is no requirement that the line should be a *straight* line; any curve which passes through the middle of the series of observations could be used. However, straight lines, implying a so-called linear trend, are much easier to handle mathematically and are most commonly used — unfortunately, more commonly than is often justified by the actual behaviour of the series.

The disadvantage of a trend line fitted in this way is its arbitrariness; no two lines fitted would be identical, except by accident. More scientifically, the line does not satisfy certain statistical criteria which have been developed for fitting trend lines.

Figure 9.3 **Monthly output from ESB generating stations (million kWh)**

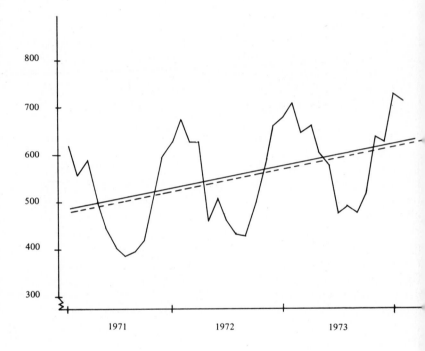

A simple method of fitting linear trend lines which does go some way towards satisfying these criteria will now be explained, using the electricity series as an example. First divide the series into two halves, taking as one half the series from January 1971 to June 1972 and as the second half the series from August 1972 to January 1974 (July 1972 is omitted so that the two sub-periods contain the same number of observations). Then calculate the mean monthly output for both sub-periods. For the period January 1971 to June 1972 this is 527.5 m kwh and for the period August 1972 to January 1974 it is 600.2 m kwh. Plot these two points on the graph, at positions corresponding to the mid-point in time of both sub-periods (between September and October 1971 for the first point and between April and May 1973 for the second point). Then join these two points by a straight line, extending the line in both directions. This is shown by the solid line on the graph. It lies a little above the freehand line, but the slopes of the two lines are remarkably similar.

This is perhaps the simplest method of fitting a trend line with any pretence of scientific method, though it can only be recommended as a very approximate estimate of trend.[7] Clearly, by extending the line on the graph, we could estimate electricity output for any future month, though a further adjustment for seasonality would have to be added, if we wished to forecast the actual, rather than the trend, value of output. This will not be discussed here.

This simple exposition of time series should enable the reader to perform certain elementary operations on series, though its more important purpose has been to provide an introduction to the basic questions and methods of approach involved in analysing time series.

---

7. The equation of this line can be written

k_c = 489.3 + 4.03t, where
k_c = expected output in kwh (trend value)
t = 0 in January 1971 and takes the values 1,2,3 . . . in successive months. Thus for February 1974, t = 37 and
k_c = 489.3 + 4.03 x 37 = 638.4

The best known method of fitting trend lines, called the *method of least squares*, yields the trend equation k_c = 493.9 + 3.70t.

SURVEY METHODS IN SOCIAL RESEARCH

MOST of the time series data and other statistics described in chapters 1-8 have been 'official' statistics — that is, statistics collected and published by government departments or other public agencies. Usually, at least in their historical origin, these statistics have been collected for some specific or general administrative purpose connected with the efficient operation of government, rather than for the purpose of scientific inquiry. Nowadays, however, it is realised that social and economic statistics have a much wider application than the original purpose which led to their collection. For example estate duty returns, which arise through the operation of tax laws, have been used to describe the structure and distribution of wealth in society, and to compare the distribution of wealth in different countries. Again, the administration of various social insurance and social assistance acts has generated a considerable volume of statistics on unemployment, and these have proved to be of great value in a large number of social and economic investigations.

Almost all research work in the social sciences which has any quantitative content — and for sound scientific reasons this is an increasing proportion — makes some use of official statistics. However, for many types of investigation it is commonly found that official statistics are not fully adequate for the purpose, and this can happen in two ways. First, the *form* in which official data are collected and published may not be suited to the particular purpose of the investigator; a good example of this in economics is that statistics of government revenue and expenditure often refer to *fiscal* years,[1] which differ from the *calendar* years used for other macro-economic data. While economists who use national accounts data almost invariably ignore this inconsistency, it would clearly be desirable that all national accounts data should relate to the same twelve-month period.

The second reason is that the data requirements of a particular investigation are often much more extensive and detailed than can be satisfied by the available official statistics. This may simply suggest that official statistics are inadequate, but, while the suggestion is often true, a more adequate supply of official statistics would never wholly meet the requirements of social scientists. It is hardly necessary to stress the point that official data collection agencies, such as the CSO, cannot be expected to anticipate and supply the full range of data − often of a somewhat arcane nature − required by current and future generations of social scientists.

This leads to the inevitable conclusion that for many purposes of research the social scientist − for subsequent reference the more general title of investigator is used − will have to collect data, and this in turn means undertaking some kind of survey. Because survey methods are so important in social research, and because the quality of such social research is strongly affected by the quality of the survey methods used, this chapter outlines the basic principles of social survey methods.

10.1 GENERAL FEATURES OF SAMPLE SURVEYS

In collecting information by means of a survey, the investigator will start by defining the specific purposes which the survey information is designed to serve. Broadly, the purpose of any survey may be classed under the heading of *estimation* or of *testing hypotheses*. In the former case, the survey information is used to infer or describe certain characteristics of interest in the population (the term 'population' will be explained below). In the latter case, the survey information is used to test the

1. In Ireland, and the UK, April-March, though since 1974 the public expenditure and revenue figures published in the Irish national accounts have been converted to a calendar year basis.

validity of a hypothesis about the population, which hypothesis may be based on earlier survey work, or *a priori* reasoning, or simply unsubstantiated belief.

Since the data requirements of a survey are determined by the objectives of the research, it is essential that these should be clearly understood and carefully specified before any attempt is made to collect data. Often, expensive survey work has been vitiated by a failure to define carefully in advance the purposes of the study and the data required to satisfy the research objectives, with the result that the wrong information, or inadequate information, has been collected.

Having defined the aims of the study, and the data necessary to carry it out, the next step is to investigate whatever data may be already available. Even if insufficient for the specific purposes of the study, the data already available may influence the type and form of information to be collected in the survey. As a common example, the forms of classification used for official census of population statistics often have a major influence on the collection and classification of survey data, since the needs of the study frequently require that the two sets of data be consistent.

The information to be acquired by the survey, and its means of collection, comprise the *design* of the survey. At the initial stage of planning the design, a number of extremely important points arise.

The first, and most basic, concerns the coverage of the survey. Suppose, for example, a survey is to be undertaken to determine the attitudes of university graduates towards employment outside Ireland, which might form part of a study on migration behaviour. Two considerations now arise. First, how do we define the *population* to which the investigation relates? Does it comprise all graduates of Irish universities, or Irish graduates only, or Irish graduates of Irish and overseas universities? How exactly is a graduate to be defined for the purpose of the study? Over what period of time should the population be defined? These, and similar questions, must be settled so that the population is precisely defined. The word population is used here in a technical sense to describe the total number of units of interest. Populations may be finite (as in this example), or infinite (such as experimental throws of a die, which in principle may be continued *ad infinitum*). Many populations are so large (in the statistical sense) that they may be considered infinite.

The second consideration is whether the investigation should cover all units of the population, once defined, or merely a *sample* of units from that population, and it is this consideration which lies at the heart of statistical inference and the development of sample survey methods. Naturally, in cases of infinite populations a sample is inevitable. Where the population is finite, however, constraints of time and cost (and, paradoxically, often accuracy, because in many cases a sample survey can be conducted more thoroughly than a full count of all the population) almost invariably lead to the choice of a sample for the investigation. On the basis of the results of the sample, statements are then made about the whole population. Clearly, if this procedure is adopted, it is vital that the sample should be 'representative' — in some defined sense — of the population from which it is drawn. The design of the sample, and the interpretation of the sample results, centres on this fundamental issue.

In selecting a sample, the main points to be decided are the size of the sample and the type of sample design to be used, by which is meant the method of sample selection. Equally important points are deciding exactly how the data are to be collected, the design and content of any questionnaires used to record the survey information, and the subsequent processing of the data from the questionnaire, which is nowadays usually done with the aid of an electronic computer. It is not feasible to give adequate coverage to all these points in the space of this chapter, and matters of questionnaire design and data processing methods will not be discussed. Instead, the following two sections will summarise the basic ideas of statistical inference which underlie sample survey methods, and the main types of sample design.

As a preliminary to this discussion one or two further points should be noted at this stage. Before undertaking the main sample survey, it is often desirable to conduct a series of preliminary tests or a small *pilot survey*. This is frequently invaluable in revealing errors and weaknesses in the coverage of the sample, in the structure and content of the questionnaire, in the determination of the final design and size of the sample, and for estimating the likely response rate, costs and time required for the main survey. A pilot survey is generally quite small, though one should if possible be flexible about its precise size, adding extra units to the pilot sample if the initial results suggest this would be a worthwhile means of improving the final design of the main survey.

Where a questionnaire is used, the results of the pilot survey almost invariably lead to modifications to the initial design and content of the questionnaire; indeed it is unwise to undertake a survey without a preliminary test of the questionnaire in this way. In addition, the results of the pilot are often the major determinant of the actual size of the main sample, a point which will be referred to in a later section of this chapter. Failure to undertake a pilot survey often causes the results of the main survey to be much less useful than they might otherwise have been – for instance a question may have been worded in such a way that the answers cannot be unambiguously interpreted, or an important question may have been omitted.

The great majority of social surveys involve the use of a structured questionnaire or record form, on which ·the survey information is recorded. Sometimes, however, survey interviews may be conducted in a different way, by means of written notes and/or tape recordings. These types of unstructured surveys usually involve lengthy 'in depth' interviews in which the personalities of the respondents and the environment of the interview are important features of the investigation. By their nature, surveys of this kind usually involve quite small samples, and the interpretation of the survey material is a more specialised (and perhaps subjective) skill, in which conventional statistical techniques are less relevant. In the ensuing discussion, however, it will be assumed that the survey involves the use of a questionnaire or record form.

A survey may be designed to collect facts, or opinions (or both), though the distinction between facts and opinion is sometimes unclear. Also, the data collected may be quantitative (for example, age, length of time employed) or qualitative (marital status, occupation). In the following section discussion of statistical inference will be generally couched in terms of factual, quantitative data, since this is most convenient for illustrative purposes. The general principles of statistical inference nevertheless apply to almost all forms of survey data, though the particular techniques applied depend upon the character of the data.

Finally, it cannot be stressed too strongly that a statistician should be consulted at the very outset of an investigation. All too often the statistician's first contact with the survey is to be presented with a mass of completed questionnaires, poorly designed and containing inadequate data for the purpose of the survey.

10.2 BASIC CONCEPTS OF SAMPLING

In the previous section it was explained that for various reasons an investigator may choose to undertake a sample survey of the population of interest, rather than include in the investigation all units in the population. For example, suppose the investigation is concerned with the pattern of expenditure of low income families, including estimation of the average weekly expenditure, and that by means of a pilot survey, and other preliminary work, definitions of 'low income families', 'weekly expenditure' and so on, have been satisfactorily resolved. The principal problems are now to determine a *method of selection* which will ensure that the sample will be 'representative' of all low income families defined by the terms of the survey, and a size of sample which will allow the investigator to estimate the average weekly expenditure of all low income families with a reasonable degree of accuracy.

In the previous chapter it was explained how a collection of data may be described by various summary measures such as the mean, the median, and the standard deviation. If the data concerned are a sample, then these summary measures are called *sample statistics*. If on the other hand the data cover all units in the population, the corresponding summary measures are called *population parameters*. The relation between sample statistics and population parameters forms the essential subject-matter of statistical inference. Often, the population parameters are unknown and the sample statistics are used as estimates of the parameters; alternatively, the sample statistics may be used to test statements, or assumptions about the population.

In what circumstances can sample statistics be used as

estimates of population parameters, and how much confidence can be attached to the accuracy of the sample measures? The answers to these questions depend on a number of factors, including the method used to select the sample. If the sample is chosen according to certain scientific principles, then measures such as the sample mean can be considered *unbiased* estimates of the corresponding population parameter.

Pursuing this further through the example suggested, suppose a list were made of all low income families, with a number attached to each family (say, 1 to 10000). Now suppose 10000 numbered tickets were thoroughly mixed up in a drum, and from this 200 tickets were drawn, as in a lottery; the families corresponding to these numbers are taken to comprise the sample. A sample drawn according to these principles is known as a *simple random sample,* and is the most basic type of sample design.[2] Its essential characteristic is that each unit in the population has an equal chance of selection in the sample.[3] Deliberate or unconscious bias in the selection of the sample is avoided.

Will the mean weekly expenditure of the 200 families in the sample (the sample mean) be equal to, or very close to, the (unknown) mean weekly expenditure of all 10000 families (the population mean)? Not necessarily, but the sample mean will be an unbiased estimate of the population mean. By chance, the sample may include a disproportionate number of 'untypical' families. By definition, however, this is unlikely; it could be reasonably expected (though it cannot be certain) that a sample of this size would reflect fairly closely the expenditure pattern of the whole population of low income families.

Suppose the numbers drawn for the sample are replaced in the drum, the tickets are thoroughly mixed up, and a second sample of 200 tickets is drawn. The families corresponding to these numbered tickets constitute a second sample (which may include some families who were also drawn in the first sample). In all likelihood, the mean weekly expenditure of the second sample will differ from the mean of the first sample, and also from the true (but unknown) population mean.

2. In practice, the process of drawing the sample is simplified by using specially-prepared tables of random numbers.
3. We avoid here the question of sampling with or without replacement.

Provided that each sample is replaced, this process of drawing random samples of 200 could be repeated indefinitely. Even if a few samples are 'untypical', the majority of samples would reflect fairly closely the expenditure characteristics of the whole population, and most of the sample means would be clustered closely around the population mean. We can therefore be reasonably confident that any one sample mean will provide a good estimate of the population mean, though there is always a chance that that sample will be 'untypical'.

The distribution of means of random samples (all of the same size) drawn from a given population is called the *sampling distribution of the mean*. A sampling distribution of the mean has the following general properties, which are stated here without proof:[4]

  (i) as the number of samples increases the *mean of the sample means* gets closer and closer to the population mean

 (ii) the sample means are distributed around the population mean in such a way that approximately fifty per cent of the sample means are equal to or less than the population mean, and fifty per cent are equal to or greater than the population mean

(iii) the greater the dispersion of values in the population, the greater the dispersion of sample means about the population mean.

Though offered without proof, these properties appeal on heuristic grounds. With repeated random sampling, it is plausible to expect roughly half the sample means to be equal to or below the population mean, and roughly half to be equal to or above the population mean. Similarly, while just through chance some sample means may be substantially lower than, and other substantially greater than, the population mean, with a large number of samples these deviations from the population mean tend to cancel out; consequently, the average of a large number of sample means should lie very close to the population mean.

With respect to (iii), consider the example of the expenditure

4. These stated properties are not universal; in particular they must be qualified or amended in regard to small samples.

of low income families. If the average weekly expenditure of each of the 10000 families in the population is roughly the same, then the means of samples drawn from that population will be very close, since the composition of each sample will make little difference. If on the other hand there is considerable variation in the average weekly expenditure of families, then the means of samples drawn from that population may vary quite significantly, owing to variations in the composition of each sample. Recall from chapter 9 that a measure of variation in a set of values is given by the *variance,* or its square root, the *standard deviation.* Thus, the greater the variance in the population, the greater the dispersion of sample means around the population mean.

Assuming for the moment that simple random sampling, as described above, constitutes the method of sample selection, the other issue to be decided is the size of the sample. Reason suggests that the larger the sample, the closer the sample mean is likely to be to the population mean. Against this has to be set the time and cost associated with a larger sample. With respect to the sampling distribution of the mean, a fourth general property can now be stated, viz.,

(iv) the greater the size of the sample, the more closely sample means will be distributed about the population mean.

Thus, for example, the means of random samples of 200 low income families will be more closely distributed around the population mean than the means of random samples of 100 low income families. Consequently, it can be argued that the mean of a sample of 200 is likely to be a more accurate estimate of the population mean than the mean of a sample of 100.

Taking properties (iii) and (iv) together, it is clear that the dispersion of sample means around the population mean is (a) directly related to the standard deviation of the population, and (b) inversely related to the size of the sample. In fact, the dispersion of sample means about the population mean can be described exactly by the following measure, called the *standard error* of the mean:

$$\sigma_{\bar{x}} = \sigma/\sqrt{n}, \text{ where}$$

$\sigma_{\bar{x}}$ = standard error of the mean

σ = standard deviation of the population
n = size of the sample

The greater the standard error, the greater the dispersion of sample means about the population mean. From the formula, it is obvious that the standard error varies directly with the standard deviation of the population and indirectly or inversely with the (square root of the) sample size.[5]

The standard error is a key measure in the application of statistical inference to sample survey methods. For the present, we will continue to assume that simple random sampling is used, and discuss the issue of the determination of sample size.

Many sample surveys follow the principle of taking as large a sample as possible within the constraints set by survey resources (usually money, or time). Though attractive on grounds of safety, this procedure is often rather wasteful. More scientifically, the investigator must strike a balance between the greater precision implied by a larger sample, and the greater cost associated with increasing the size of the sample. In many types of industrial or scientific survey work, this 'trade-off' between cost and precision can be expressed in financial or other quantitative terms, and an optimal size of sample determined.[6] In most social survey work, the criteria for determining an optimal size are much more subjective, though the same principles apply. These will now be explained with reference to the example quoted previously.

Suppose the aim is to estimate the average weekly expenditure of all low income families. An exact estimate of the population mean can only be guaranteed by including every family in the sample (which would then be a full count), which can be assumed to be impractical. The real question is how precise we wish the sample estimate to be.

Assume that the survey is to be undertaken on behalf of a government department, who specify that the sample mean estimate must be within plus or minus ten pence of the true (unknown) population mean. It is now required to draw a sample large enough to be confident that the sample mean will

5. This formula has to be modified in the case of a finite population, though it can be held to apply in the case of large populations, for which the sample size is a very small fraction of the total population.

6. In quality control work, for example, the cost of testing product samples can be compared with the probable financial cost incurred if a faulty batch gets through.

lie within the range plus or minus ten pence of the population mean.

To determine the sample size appropriate for these requirements, the investigator will make use of certain additional properties of the sampling distribution of the mean and its standard error. Denoting the population mean by the symbol μ, one of these properties can be expressed as follows, with respect to repeated random samples of size n;

(v) approximately 95 per cent of sample means will lie within the range plus or minus two standard errors of the population mean.

If repeated random samples of size n are drawn from a population, then approximately 95 per cent of the sample means will lie within two standard errors of the population mean.

As another property,

(vi) approximately 99 per cent of sample means will lie within the range plus or minus 2.6 standard errors[7] of the population mean.

More generally, a range can be specified for any percentage of sample means up to, *but not including,* 100 per cent.[8]

If he knows the standard deviation of the population, the investigator can now fix the size of the sample, by means of an elementary calculation, to be confident (but not certain) that the sample mean will lie within ten pence of the true population mean. He reasons as follows:

(a) from property (vi), note that 99 per cent of sample means lie within the range 2.6 standard errors of the population mean

(b) the requirement of the survey is that 2.6 standard errors = 10 pence

(c) standard error = $\sigma_{\bar{x}} = \sigma/\sqrt{n}$, so it is required that $2.6 \, \sigma/\sqrt{n} = 10$

7. More precisely, in the case of the so-called normal distribution of sample means, 95 per cent of sample means will lie within the range $\mu \pm 1.96$ standard errors, and 99 per cent of sample means will lie within the range $\mu \pm 2.58$ standard errors.

8. In statistical language, the sampling distribution of the mean is asymptotic. This means that the full range of sample means is indeterminate, though it can be specified up to 99.99 . . . %.

(d) if the population standard deviation is known, this little equation can be solved for n. Suppose $\sigma = 50$, then

$$2.6 \times 50/\sqrt{n} = 10$$
i.e. $\quad 130 = 10\sqrt{n}$
i.e. $\quad \sqrt{n} = 13$
i.e. $\quad n = 169$

and the required sample size is at least 169.

In fact, since the population mean is unknown, it is probable that the population standard deviation will also be unknown. Obtaining an estimate of the standard deviation is one of the purposes of the pilot survey. In this case, the sample size calculated should be regarded as a minimum requirement.

The investigator can now be reasonably confident that, by taking a sample of 169, the sample mean will lie within ten pence of the population mean. He cannot be certain, because approximately one per cent of the means of random samples of size 169 fall *outside* the range $\mu \pm 2.6$ standard errors, and by chance the sample actually selected may be one of these one per cent. By definition, however, the probability of this happening is small.

By similar reasoning based on property (v), the reader can estimate that the sample size required is about 100. However, with this size of sample there is a greater risk of the sample mean falling outside the specified range; with repeated sampling, approximately 5 per cent of sample means would lie more than ten pence from the population mean, and by chance the sample actually selected may be one of these.

Clearly, the size of sample selected depends on how much importance is attached to the ten pence limits imposed. If, as in many social surveys, the degree of precision required is determined in a rather subjective way, the sample size of 100 would probably be considered acceptable. However, if the degree of precision implied by the ten pence limit is regarded as important, the sample of 169 would be preferable, since the risk of the sample mean estimate falling outside these limits is small — one per cent. By increasing the sample size beyond 169, the risk could be further reduced, though survey costs would increase.[9]

9. For example, the size of sample required to ensure that 99.5 per cent of sample means fall within the range $\mu \pm 10$ pence is, in this example, about 200.

Suppose a sample size of 100 is decided on. The sample is selected and the sample mean is calculated; suppose this turns out to be £18.50. Following the convention established in chapter 9, this can be written $\bar{x} = 18.50$.

The sample mean of 18.50 is an unbiased estimate of the (unknown) population mean. How good an estimate is it? From property (v), it is known that 95 per cent of sample means will lie within the range μ + or - 2.6 standard errors, and the size of sample has been fixed to ensure that this yields $\mu \pm 10$ pence. Now, if 95 per cent of sample means lie within the range $\mu \pm 10$ pence, it follows that, in 95 per cent of samples, the population mean will lie within the range $\bar{x} \pm 10$ pence. In 5 per cent of cases, μ will lie outside the range $\bar{x} \pm 10$ pence. We can, therefore, be '95 per cent confident' that the population mean will lie within the range $\bar{x} \pm 10$ pence. With $\bar{x} = £18.50$, it can be concluded

(a) that £18.50 is the best estimate of the population mean, and
(b) that we can be 95 per cent confident that the population mean falls between £18.50 $\pm$ 10 pence, or £18.40 – £18.60.

Applying the same reasoning with respect to property (vi), approximately 99 per cent of sample means will lie within the range $\mu \pm 2.6$ standard errors.

i.e. $\mu \pm 2.6 \; \sigma_{\bar{x}}$
i.e. $\mu \pm 2.6 \; \sigma/\sqrt{n}$
i.e. $\mu \pm 2.6 \times 50/\sqrt{100}$
i.e. $\mu \pm 13.0$ pence

By corresponding reasoning, since 99 per cent of sample means fall within the range $\mu \pm 13.0$ pence, in 99 per cent of cases μ will lie within the range $\bar{x} \pm 13.0$ pence. With $\bar{x} = £18.50$, this gives a '99 per cent confidence interval' of £18.37 to £18.63. Increased confidence about the range within which μ falls requires a wider 'confidence interval'.

Having explained in simple terms the application of statistical inference to the determination of sample size, and to questions of estimation, its application to tests of hypotheses will be briefly explained. There are many different types of such tests, which are frequently described as 'tests of significance'. To simplify the exposition, the following hypothetical example is also concerned with the expenditures of low income families.

In this case, suppose it is known that the mean weekly expenditure of all low income families is £18.55 and that the standard deviation is fifty pence. A random sample of 64 low income families from a particular constituency reveals a mean weekly expenditure of £18.30 and the opposition TD for this constituency asserts that this 'proves' that low income families in his constituency have an average weekly expenditure different from the national average. Does the evidence support this assertion?

From property (v), it is known that approximately 95 per cent of sample means will be distributed about the population mean within the range $\mu \pm 2$ standard errors. With a population mean of £18.55, a population standard deviation of 50 pence, and a sample size of 64, this gives the '95 per cent confidence interval' as

$$£18.55 \pm 2.0 \times 50/\sqrt{64}$$
i.e. $£18.55 \pm 12.5$ pence
i.e. £18.425 to £18.675

The investigator now reasons as follows. To begin with, he sets up the hypothesis that there is no difference between the average level of expenditure of all low income families, and the average level of expenditure of low income families in the particular constituency concerned. This is called the *null hypothesis,* and asserts that the difference between the sample mean and the population mean arises simply by chance.

If the null hypothesis were true, the investigator could be 95 per cent confident that any given sample mean (based on a sample of 64) would fall within the range £18.42 and £18.68, as calculated above. However, the mean of the sample concerned is £18.30, which falls outside this range. There are two alternative explanations for this (assuming the sample to be an unbiased random sample).

(a) The null hypothesis is true but we have struck one of the 5 per cent of sample means which fall outside the 95 per cent range.

(b) The average level of expenditure of low income families

in this constituency is different from (in this case lower than) the national average for low income families. By definition, the first explanation is unlikely, and the second is accepted. It is concluded that the average weekly expenditure of low income families in that constituency is significantly lower than the national average for low income families. The evidence supports the TD's contention, though it does not prove it beyond doubt, since the possibility of a statistical fluke — the first alternative explanation — cannot be ruled out.

Even more conclusive, property (vi) tells us that the '99% confidence interval' for this example is £18.55 ± 2.6 x 50/$\sqrt{64}$

    i.e.   £18.55 ± 16.25 pence
    i.e.   £18.38 to £18.72 approximately.

If the null hypothesis were true, 99 per cent of sample means would be expected to fall within this range. The sample mean falls outside this range, and the null hypothesis is again rejected. It is still possible that we have struck a fluke, but even more unlikely, since there is less than one chance in a hundred that the null hypothesis is correct.[10]

Obviously, there will be cases in which the 95 per cent confidence interval suggests rejection of the null hypothesis, while the 99 per cent confidence interval suggests acceptance. In the example quoted, a value of £18.40 would have fallen outside the 95 per cent confidence interval, but inside the 99 per cent interval. Usually, rejection at the 95 per cent level is considered sufficient, but this depends on the relative costs of (a) wrongly rejecting, or (b) wrongly accepting the null hypothesis. Alternatively, a second sample could be taken, though this is not always feasible.

This concludes our brief review of the basic concepts of statistical inference, which of necessity has been highly simplified. In particular, it should be noted that the properties of sampling distributions listed here have been based on a number of (unstated) assumptions about the nature of the population from which the sampling distribution is derived. It is therefore unwise to assume that these properties hold in particular cases,

10. Strictly, a so-called 'one-tailed' test would have been appropriate here, but the result would have been the same.

without further investigation. However, the preceding discussion is intended to provide some insight into the general principles of sampling techniques.

10.3 TYPES OF SAMPLE DESIGN

In the preceding section, sampling distributions and applications of statistical inference were discussed on the assumption that the sample was selected by means of a *simple random sample,* the essence of which is that each unit in the population has an equal chance of selection. Although this is the most basic and best known type of sample design, other types of sample design are often preferred on theoretical and/or practical grounds. Some of these designs will now be briefly described.

Whatever the sample design, the most important characteristic to be preserved is that of randomness in the selection of the sample, though in practice many samples do not meet this requirement. The calculation of standard errors and the application of tests of significance and estimation are valid only if the sample has been selected randomly, and randomness is a necessary, though not sufficient, condition for unbiased sample estimates.

The selection of a random sample presupposes a list of the population from which the sample is to be chosen; this list is called the sampling *frame.* Often, obtaining a frame is a major source of difficulty, since such a list may not be already available and it may be impractical or impossible to prepare one.[11] We return to this point below. If a ready-made frame is available, or has been constructed, a random sample can be drawn, for example using specially prepared tables of random numbers. Here, a sequence of numbers is read off the random number tables and the corresponding units in the population (the frame is also numbered) comprise the sample.

It is intuitively obvious that if a sample is drawn in this way, each unit in the population has an equal chance of selection. This then is a simple random sample. However, while preserving randomness in the selection process, it is possible to introduce

11. A complete list or frame is not always a necessary prerequisite for drawing a random sample – and obviously does not apply in the case of an infinite population – but it is usually required in social surveys.

certain restrictions or qualifications to the procedure, with the aim of improving the character of the sample.

The best-known variant of the simple random sample is the *stratified random sample*. The population is divided into different classes or groups and a random sample is selected from each class (stratum). The sub-samples from each stratum are then combined to form the total sample. For example, suppose the population of interest was the total labour force. This might be stratifed by occupation, and a random sample selected from each occupational group. The occupational samples are then combined to form the total sample.

Without pursuing the argument in detail, the justification for stratifying the sampling frame is that the standard error of the mean (and the standard error of other sample statistics) from a stratified random sample will often be less than the standard error of the mean from a simple random sample of the same size. One obvious feature of a stratified random sample is that the investigator can control the proportion in which each stratum is represented in the sample. For instance, the investigator could ensure that the proportions in which the various strata are represented in the sample are identical to the proportions in which these strata are represented in the total population. Thus, for example, if twelve per cent of the total labour force are electricians, twelve per cent of the sample would be electricians, and similarly for other occupational groups. In this way, the occupational composition of the sample would reflect exactly the occupational composition of the population.

In a simple random sample, there is no guarantee that the composition of the sample, in terms of various groups or strata, will reflect the composition of the population. This introduces a random element of variability in a simple random sample which is not present in a stratified random sample; as a result the standard errors of statistics derived from a stratified random sample are frequently (although not invariably) less than those derived from a simple random sample of the same size.

Paradoxically, the optimal design for a stratified random sample does not necessarily require that each stratum should be represented in the sample in the same proportion as in the total population. A simple though extreme example may illustrate this point. Suppose the object was to estimate the mean length of stay of all patients passing through Dublin hospitals over a certain period, and it was decided to do this by means of a stratified random sample of patients, the factor of stratification being type of illness. All patients would then be classified by illness and a random sample selected from each stratum, to make up the total sample. Suppose however it was known that for one form of illness — say measles — length of stay in hospital was invariably the same for all patients. Then it would only be necessary to select a sample of *one* from this stratum to determine average length of stay for measles patients. For coronary heart disease, on the other hand, a large sample would be desirable if length of stay for this category of patients were highly variable.

In this case, the sample composition would not reflect the population composition in terms of the number of patients in each category, but would be proportional to the variability (or variance) in length of stay in each stratum. Strata with a high variance would be 'over-represented' in the sample and strata with a low variance would be 'under-represented'. It was explained in the previous section that the standard error of a sample is directly related to the standard deviation of the parent population, and inversely related to the sample size. In the case of a stratified random sample the formula is a little more complicated, being a weighted average of the standard errors for each stratum, but the essential point is that the standard error of the total sample can be minimised if the composition of the sample is related to the standard deviation of each stratum, rather than to its size.

One obvious implication of this procedure is that each unit in the population no longer has an equal chance of selection in the sample. If two strata are the same size but have different standard deviations, a unit in the stratum with the greater standard deviation will have a greater chance of selection than a unit in the other stratum. It is often thought that this vitiates the principle of random sampling, but this is not so. It is only necessary that the units *within* each stratum should have an equal chance of selection, and that each unit in the population should have a known (non-zero) probability of selection. In simple random sampling this probability is the same for each unit. In a stratified random sample, each unit has an equal chance of selection only if the same sampling fraction is applied to each stratum — this is called a *uniform sampling fraction*.[12] In the example cited above, where the sample composition was proportional to the standard deviation of each stratum, a *variable sampling fraction* is applied; the probability of selection is the same *within,* but not *between* strata.

Note that when a variable sampling fraction is used, the sample statistics have to be weighted to reflect the relative importance of each stratum in the population. The sample mean, for instance, will be calculated as a weighted average of the means of each stratum, the weights being the proportions in which each stratum is represented in the whole population.

Before leaving stratification, two further points may be mentioned. First, the criteria used for stratification must be associated with the variables or attributes of interest in the survey, otherwise there is no gain in stratification. Thus, in investigating length of stay in hospital, there would be no point in stratifying patients by type of illness unless it were believed that type of illness had some bearing on length of stay. Often, this kind of association can only be discovered or confirmed by means of a pilot survey.

Secondly, more than one factor of stratification can be used. To pursue the same example, if it were discovered that age as well as type of illness influenced length of stay, it would be desirable to stratify the sample by both age and type of illness, so increasing the number of distinct strata.

It was remarked above that a practical difficulty in many sample surveys is the absence of a frame from which the sample is selected. Sometimes, of course, the defined population is relatively small and a frame can be constructed by the investigator without too much difficulty — for example the population of students at a particular college or university. In many instances, however, the population is so large (for example, the adult population of the country), or of such a nature that no frame is available and it is simply unfeasible to construct one. In these

12. If S_i is the size of sample to be selected from the i th stratum, and P_i the population of that stratum, the sampling fraction is S_i/P_i. A uniform sampling fraction is such that S/P is the same for all i.

circumstances, investigators either avoid using a frame, or have recourse to a 'ready-made' frame, such as the electoral register, telephone directories, lists maintained by government departments, and a miscellany of other sources which might be assumed to approximate to the population of interest. For national surveys in which persons or households comprise the population of interest, the electoral register is a well-used source. The register purports to include the names and addresses of all those aged 18 and over who are entitled to vote in local and Dail elections; it is readily available, and is updated annually. Other advantages are that names are organised by area (down to street level), and are numbered, which makes the register convenient for sampling. Limitations of the register as a frame are that it excludes those not entitled to vote, or who have not bothered to register; also, in areas in which there is a high turnover of population, the register may become quickly out of date. For these reasons the electoral register is never likely to correspond exactly to the population defined by the survey, and a sample selected from the register will therefore contain some element of bias. Despite these limitations, for many types of survey work the register is the best ready-made frame available, though the proportion of the eligible population who do not register, and the possible nature of the bias in the sample resulting from this, should not be overlooked.

Another well-known type of sample design is *multi-stage sampling* (which is often combined with stratification). Suppose it is required to undertake a survey of households, and preliminary investigation suggests that a sample of about 2000 households is required. Supposing an adequate sampling frame of all households in the country to be available, a simple random sample could be selected and the data collection process set in motion. However, in all likelihood such a sample of households would be scattered throughout the country, and data collection would be very expensive and time-consuming.

As an alternative, the investigator could begin by drawing up a list of, say, Dail constituencies, from which a simple random sample (or stratified random sample) could be drawn. The constituencies selected in this way − suppose there are three of them − constitute the first stage sample units.

Next, a list is prepared of all the wards or district electoral divisions contained in the three first-stage sample units, and a simple or stratified random sample is selected from this list. The electoral areas chosen represent the second-stage sample units.

The third-stage sampling frame would comprise the polling districts contained within the second-stage units, and a random sample would be selected from this list of polling districts. At this stage, depending on the exact design of the sample, the final sample might be taken to comprise all the households contained within these third-stage sample units; alternatively, a further stage of selecting a sample of households included in these polling districts might be undertaken.

The most obvious advantage of multi-stage sampling[13] is that it concentrates survey resources, particularly in cases where the population is dispersed over a wide geographical area, while at the same time maintaining the principles of random selection. To ensure a 'representative' coverage at the final stage, stratification is commonly used at each stage. For instance, in the case of area sampling quoted above it would be generally undesirable (though of course this would depend upon the purpose of the survey) to end up with a sample comprising purely rural (or alternatively purely urban) households, and the sample units would be stratified at each stage to ensure that this did not happen.

Another important advantage of multi-stage sampling is that the investigator can avoid the need for a comprehensive sampling frame of final units. In the example above, we require only an enumeration of households contained within the third-stage sample units (the polling districts). This is clearly a considerable advantage; in many cases an adequate ready-made sampling frame does not exist, and to construct one may be impossible or formidably expensive of survey resources.

Another type of sample design which is widely used in market research and opinion poll surveys is *quota sampling*. The most significant characteristic of quota sampling is that it is non-random; the sample is selected by the interviewer, rather

---

13. A particular case of multi-stage sampling is 'cluster' sampling, in which the process stops after the first stage; there is a complete enumeration or random sample of all final units contained within the first-stage sample units.

than by strictly random methods from a sampling frame. This feature of quota sampling has been (and continues to be) the subject of controversy and criticism, since interviewer selection introduces an unknown element of bias, and the principles of statistical inference outlined in the previous section of this chapter are not strictly applicable to the results of a quota sample.

In quota sampling, a fixed number of respondents are selected by the interviewer (in the street, at home, at work, and so on, according to certain rules prescribed by the investigator) with reference to a predetermined matrix of *quota controls.* These controls correspond to stratification factors used in stratified random sampling; almost invariably, they include age, sex, and socio-economic status as controls. Thus, for example, an interviewer may be allocated a quota of twenty-five people to select, of whom ten must be females; each sex cohort must also satisfy other criteria with respect to socio-economic status and age. Thus, one of the respondents must be a woman aged 20-29, from socio-economic class D, for example, and the other respondents will be defined in similar terms. Other criteria, such as occupation, may also be involved. Like stratification, these quota controls are designed to ensure a predetermined composition of the sample.

Exactly how the interviewer selects the sample — subject to the quota controls — depends on instructions and rules laid down by the investigator, but however carefully designed to minimise bias in selection, the resulting sample is not a random sample.

It is not intended here to elaborate the arguments for and against quota sampling (a good summary is given in Moser [1]). Its principal advantages are cost, speed and the fact that a sampling frame is not required. Its main disadvantage is its non-random character, which makes it more difficult to assess the significance of the results of a quota sample.

In most types of survey work, the census of population data are an important reference source. As explained in chapter 1, the census provides a detailed demographic and socio-economic profile of the population at certain dates; the census data, and the forms of classification used in the published reports, influence the design of sample surveys, the definitions used, and the interpretation of survey data. Often, census data provide the 'weights' to be applied to survey data, and a means of assessing the 'representativeness' of the sample. In stratifying area samples, for instance, census data will generally be used for allocating area sample units to particular strata, and will also indicate the fraction of total population included within each stratum.

This concludes our brief and summary review of the principal types of sample design used in social survey work. For a more comprehensive discussion, an excellent source is Moser (see p.197).

10.4   SAMPLE SURVEYS IN PRACTICE

Sample survey methods are widely used in Ireland for purposes of scientific research (including the social sciences), by business firms interested in market research, and by government, though the use of sample surveys to expand the range of official statistics in Ireland is much less than it might be.

As implied or stated in earlier chapters, the extent and quality of official social statistics in Ireland leave much to be desired. The use of sample surveys lies mainly in the area of economic statistics. A number of important series of economic statistics published regularly in the *Irish Statistical Bulletin,* including some series referred to in this book, are based on sample data. They include the data used to construct index numbers of retail sales and the consumer price index, the results of the quarterly industrial production inquiry, various series of agricultural prices, and the passenger card inquiry, which is used to estimate the numbers and expenditure of visitors to Ireland and Irish visitors abroad. In some cases — for example the annual enumeration of crops and livestock, and the census of distribution — a full count is conducted at intervals of some years, while sample data are used for intervening years. This is a particularly useful application of sampling methods for generating series. A regular series can be established without the commitment of resources required to conduct a full count on each occasion, while the taking of a full count at intervals provides a check on the accuracy of the sample data series, and can be used to update the sampling frame.

One of the best-known examples of government sample

surveys is the household budget inquiry, which was discussed in chapter 7. The inquiry is carried out at intervals by the CSO, and is primarily designed to obtain information on expenditure patterns, which can be used as 'weights' in the construction of the consumer price index. (The HBI data also serve many other uses.)

The 1965-66 inquiry was based on a sample of nearly 4800 urban households,[14] using a stratified cluster sampling design. First-stage units were all towns and villages in Ireland, which were stratified into six size categories according to population. From these a sample of 65 towns and villages was selected, including all towns with a population of more than 10000 inhabitants and, at the other end of the scale, 1 in 32 villages with a population of less than 500. At the next stage, a random sample of households was selected from the population of households included in the areas defined by the 65 first-stage sample units; the actual numbers of households selected in each town or village (the sampling fraction) was fixed to satisfy the overall requirement that each urban household had an equal chance of selection for the sample. In the case of the larger urban areas, the electoral register served as the sampling frame, while in other areas the sampling frame was the list of heads of households compiled in the 1961 census of population (modified where possible to allow for changes between 1961 and 1965).

This sampling procedure — a detailed description of which is given in the HBI Report — yielded a total of 6000 private urban households (approximately 1 in 60 of all urban households), which for fieldwork purposes were divided into 18 'zones' or areas. A carefully-ordered list of sample households was drawn up for each zone, and interviewers were instructed to obtain a specific quota of co-operating households in each zone, approaching households in the order determined by the lists. The quota for each zone was set so as to obtain a target sample of 2400 households for the first phase of the inquiry. Co-operating households were asked to keep a detailed record of expenditure over a period of fourteen successive days, as well as providing various additional data on income and household composition.

14. The 1973 inquiry was extended to include rural households, a substantial improvement in the usefulness of the inquiry.

For the second phase of the inquiry, six months later, those households who had participated in the first phase were again asked to co-operate for a further fourteen-day period, as were also those households which, though approached, had not participated in the first phase. Ninety-three per cent of those who had co-operated in the first phase agreed to co-operate in the second; a further one per cent of the second-phase sample target of 2400 were drawn from those who had been approached but who had not participated in the first phase. The remaining six per cent of the second-phase sample were drawn from those sample households which had not been previously approached.

In all, 4214 of the 6000 sample households were actually approached; 4771 returns were obtained (2398 in the first phase, 2373 in the second), of which twelve were discarded as unsatisfactory. It should be noted that, for the purposes of the analysis, 'the same household participating in both fieldwork cycles was regarded as two separate households', so that the results of the inquiry are taken to be based on a sample of 4759 households. (For elaboration of this assumption, see the text of the HBI Report.) A further point to note is that in the presentation of results, sample data have been adjusted, whenever appropriate, to account for the non-proportionate composition of sample households. Following the data collection, respondent households were stratified by household size (four groups), social class (six groups) and size of town or village (four groups) yielding a matrix of 96 (4 x 4 x 6) categories of sample households. The relative numbers of sample households in each category were then compared with the relative numbers of all households in each category. This comparison was used to derive 'grossing factors' which could be applied to sample data to correct for categories of households which were over-represented or under-represented in the sample. In this way, the adjusted sample data can be said to be more representative of the total population of urban households.

A notable amount of sample survey work, usually designed and carried out by specialist market research organisations, is commissioned by business firms, though naturally the results of such research are seldom available for general readership. This work is mainly concerned with studies of consumer behaviour and attitudes, as an aid to the marketing of consumer goods and services (or, less frequently, industrial goods and services). Though primarily oriented towards marketing, however, these surveys often contain material of interest to the social scientist. An excellent example is the *Joint National Media Research Survey* conducted by Irish Marketing Surveys Limited.[15] This is a continuous sample survey of households, sponsored by a consortium of Irish newspaper publishers, RTE, cinema interests and advertising agencies, and its primary interest is the reading, television-viewing, and cinema-going habits of the population. This information is itself interesting, but in addition the *JNMR* reports contain a great deal of data on other social and economic characteristics of the population, including smoking and drinking habits, holidays, ownership of vehicles and other consumer durables, and saving and banking habits. The *JNMR* survey is based on a cluster sampling design; the basic sampling frame is the electoral register, from which a random sample of addresses are drawn (having first selected the sample areas); an adult member of the household living at each address is then selected for interview. This type of sampling procedure is described more fully below. Over 5 000 interviews were carried out for the 1974/75 survey, which is a very satisfactory sample size for population estimates of the type included in this survey.[16]

Apart from regular or continuous sample survey work carried out by government and market research agencies, there is a large and growing volume of survey work carried out in Ireland in connection with specific research projects in the social sciences. It is impossible to review or even list the many published items of research which have utilised sample survey methods, but the references cited at the end of this chapter may be found of interest as examples of the use of survey techniques and sample design.

An example which excited a wide public interest was the *Report on Public Preference for a Second Television Channel*, undertaken by Irish Marketing Surveys for the Minister for Posts and Telegraphs, and Radio Telefis Eireann. The object of

15. See also chapter 8, section 8.3.
16. The failure rate is apparently very low.

the survey was to assess the public's preference for a second television channel which would be broadcast throughout the Republic — either a rebroadcast of the BBC-1 Northern Ireland service, or a mixture of BBC-2, BBC-3, ITV and some home-produced programmes, the material to be selected and presented by RTE.

The assessment was carried out by means of a sample survey of adults (persons aged eighteen and over) in the Republic. Those selected for the sample were interviewed and a simple questionnaire was completed by the interviewer in respect of each respondent. Altogether 2 124 successful interviews were completed, from an initial sample of 2 420 addresses — a 'success rate' of 87.7 per cent.

Prior to the main survey, a pilot study was undertaken. One of the purposes of the pilot was to determine the form in which the main question at issue — the preference for either type of second channel — was to be presented to the respondent. As a result, it was decided to summarise the argument for each channel on a card, to be given to the respondent to read at an appropriate point during the interview.

In terms of the types of sample design discussed earlier in this chapter, this particular sample survey corresponded to a stratified cluster sample.

First-stage sampling units comprised areas approximately equivalent to district electoral divisions (or groups of district electoral divisions), which were stratified by area, whether urban or rural, and by reception area — i.e. whether single channel or multi-channel reception area for television broadcasting. Two hundred and twenty first-stage sampling units were selected from the total frame, which is a large selection by ordinary standards, justified by the importance of obtaining a widely distributed, and hence more obviously representative, sample of households throughout the country.

Second-stage sampling units were selected from the electoral registers corresponding to the 220 first-stage sample units (areas). Although electors were chosen from the register, they were regarded as a sample of households or addresses; the person selected from the register was not necessarily the person selected for the interview, who might be any person (aged eighteen or over) residing in that household. At the interview with the contact,[17] the names of all persons aged eighteen and over in the household were recorded, and by means of a simple predetermined decision rule, the interviewer selected one person in the household to be interviewed. This determined the final-stage sample units.

Results of the survey were analysed by region, sex, age, and socio-economic group. For the country as a whole, 62 per cent of the sample expressed a preference for the RTE-2 channel, while 35 per cent opted for BBC-1 (1 per cent said 'Neither', and there were 2 per cent of 'Don't Know'). While there was relatively little variation between groups, a stronger preference for BBC-1 was expressed by younger people, the middle classes, and those living in single-channel areas (particularly in Cork, Limerick and Galway). In all major groups, however, a clear majority preferred RTE-2. The survey report includes a succinct description of the design and methodology of the survey.

Another survey which employed a stratified cluster sampling design was the Institute of Public Administration report, *A Study of Attitudes towards the Executive Officer Grade in the Civil Service*. The terms of reference of this study laid particular emphasis on attitudes amongst secondary school pupils, the teachers and parents of such pupils, persons aged nineteen to twenty-seven who would be eligible to compete in the open executive officer competition, and executive officers already recruited for the civil service who had two to four years experience. It can be seen therefore that the study was concerned with a number of distinct groups in the population. The Department of the Public Service commissioned the study because it was experiencing increasing difficulty in recruiting executive officers, and because it considered that, to improve recruitment and recruitment procedures, it was important to assess the current attitudes of those in the population from whom future executive officers would be drawn, and also the attitudes of related groups such as parents and teachers.

Part I of the research report describes the methodology. There is an interesting description of the pilot survey of school

17. The contacts were chosen from the register by a method known as systematic sampling. For most purposes this can be treated as equivalent to simple random sampling. In fact, once the household was selected, any responsible person in the household could serve as the contact.

pupils (the most important group in the study), results of which were used in the design and content of a questionnaire; and of the pre-testing of the questionnaire on a further sample of pupils, results of which were used in the final design of the questionnaire and in the development of appropriate descriptive terms and statistical measures. A small pilot study of executive officers was also undertaken.

For the main sample of school pupils, the population of interest was defined as pupils studying for the leaving certificate who had attained a specified minimum academic standard in the intermediate certificate examination. As already explained, a stratified cluster sample design was used, the first-stage units being secondary schools. The schools were stratified to reflect certain demographic characteristics — for example to achieve a balance of urban and rural schools in the sample — and a stratified random sample of seventy schools was selected, of which fifty-five agreed to participate in the study.

In schools with ten or fewer eligible pupils (eligible, that is, in terms of the criteria defining the population), all eligible pupils were included in the sample. In schools with more than ten eligible pupils, a random sample of ten was selected. This process yielded a total sample of 509 pupils, from which 445 completed returns were obtained.

The sample of teachers was also selected from the fifty-five participating schools. From the list of leaving certificate teachers in each school, five were selected for interview (the selection was purposive rather than random). Two hundred and fifty returns were obtained from a sample of 275 teachers.

The third group falling within the terms of reference of the study were persons with post-secondary school experience, aged nineteen to twenty-seven, who would be eligible to enter the open competition for executive officers. No available sampling frame existed for this population, and for the purposes of the study it was decided to select a sample from amongst the undergraduate populations of University College Cork, University College Dublin, and University College Galway. Unfortunately, it was apparently not possible to obtain a list of undergraduates at each institution, from which a random sample could be selected; instead the sample comprised volunteers from classes in arts, science and commerce. In this way 177 returns were obtained. This particular sample therefore suffered two defects. First, the sample was not drawn from the whole population of persons aged nineteen to twenty-seven with appropriate academic qualifications, but only from a sub-group of that population. Secondly, the sample was self-selected, comprising only volunteers. The extent to which these defects may bias the results of this part of the study is, of course, a matter of judgement, but certainly the results relating to this group must be treated with some caution. (It should be added that social surveys in practice commonly fail to conform strictly to theoretical sampling requirements, frequently because of the difficulty in obtaining or constructing adequate sampling frames.)

Finally, from serving executive officers with two to four years experience a sample of 169 was selected, from which 127 usable returns were obtained.

Data from these samples provided the basis for the analysis. For details of the analysis, and the conclusions and recommendations, the reader is referred to the report, which provides a good example of the application of survey methods in social investigation, and the subsequent application of techniques of statistical analysis to survey data.

REFERENCES

For a non-mathemtical introduction to survey methods and principles of statistical inference, an excellent reference is
[1] C.A. Moser, *Survey Methods in Social Investigation* (second edition) London: Heinemann, 1971
For the more mathematically inclined, there are a large number of books on statistical inference. A useful introductory text is
[2] K.A. Yeomans, *Statistics for the Social Scientist: 2 Applied Statistics*, Harmondsworth: Penguin, 1968
while at a more advanced level a good text is
[3] E.S. Keeping, *An Introduction to Statistical Inference,* New York: Van Nostrand Reinhold, 1962

References cited in this chapter were
[4] Household Budget Inquiry 1965/66, CSO, 1969, Dublin: Stationery Office

[5] *Joint National Media Research 1974/75,* Dublin: Irish Marketing Surveys, 1975
[6] *Report on Public Preference for a Second Television Channel,* Dublin: Irish Marketing Surveys, 1975
[7] J. McGowan, M. Franklin, M. Fine and M. Moore, *A Study of Attitudes towards the Executive Officer Grade in the Civil Service,* Dublin: Institute of Public Administration, 1974

Other references which provide useful examples of sample survey methods include

[8] H. Behrend, A. Knowles, and J. Davies, *Views on Pay Increases, Fringe Benefits and Low Pay,* Economic and Social Research Institute Paper No. 56, 1970
[9] M.J. Harrison, and S. Nolan, 'The Distribution of Personal Wealth in Ireland — A Comment', *Economic and Social Review*, VII, 1, October 1975
[10] I. Hart, 'Absenteeism at National School — Educational Medical and Social Aspects'. *Economic and Social Review*, VI, 3, April 1975
[11] I. Hart, and B. O'Sullivan, 'Inter-Generational Social Mobility and Individual Differences among Dubliners', *Economic and Social Review*, II, 1, October 1970
[12] B. Hutchinson, 'Social Status and Inter-Generational Social Mobility in Dublin', Economic and Social Research Institute Paper No. 48. 1969
[13] P.M. Lyons, 'The Distribution of Personal Wealth in Ireland' in J. Bristow and A.A.Tait (eds), *Ireland: Problems of a Developing Economy,* Dublin: Gill and Macmillan, 1972
[14] M. MacGreil, 'Religious beliefs and practice of Dublin adults', *Social Studies*, III, 2, April 1974
[15] Market Research Bureau of Ireland, 'Views on Contraception and Divorce', *Social Studies*, III, 3, June 1974
[16] J. Rudd, 'A Survey of National School Terminal Leavers', *Social Studies,* I, 2, January 1972
[17] A. Sheehy and R. O'Connor, *Rural Household Budget — Feasibility Study,* Economic and Social Research Institute Paper No. 61, 1971
[18] B.M. Walsh, and A. O'Toole, *Women and Employment in Ireland: Results of a National Survey,* Economic and

Social Research Institute Paper No. 69, 1973
[19] K. Wilson-Davies, 'Irish Attitudes to Family Planning', *Social Studies*, III, 3, June 1974

INDEX

accidents, 51
advertising, 133,134
age specific death rate, 18,20,
21-22, 39-40,43
allowances, 92
arithmetic mean, 142-44,145-
47
assistance
social, 82-83,87-92
unemployment, 83-87
attribute, 142
average
arithmetic mean, 142-44,
145-47
moving, 160-64

benefit
disability, 91
disablement, 90
unemployment, 83-87
birth rates, 23-28

car registrations, 112
census of population, 1-14,25,
28-31
as reference source for
sample surveys, 189-90
education survey in, 76-77
housing survey in, 61-66

importance in population
forecasting, 7
children
allowances, 92
health of, 51
communications, 133-35,
193-95
Consumer Price Index, 117-22
consumption expenditure,
107-12
continuous variable, 142
crude birth rate, 23
crude death rate, 17-18, 21-
22, 37
cyclical fluctuations, 158-59,
163-64

death rates, 17-23,36-46
demography, chapters 1 and 2
passim
dental services, 52
disability benefit, 91
disablement benefit, 90
discrete variable, 142
dispersion, measures of,
147-49
distribution of income, 101-04,
107
distribution of wealth, 104-07,

dwellings
  begun and authorised, 60
  completed, 58-60

earnings surveys, 101-02
education, 12, chapter 5
elderly
  health of, 50-51
  pensions for, 87-90
elections, 128-31
electoral register, 129
  use as sampling frame, 187
emigrants, 29-30
expenditure patterns, 111

Family Expenditure Survey
  (UK), 123-24
fertility
  census inquiry, 11
  rates, 23-28
frequency distributions
  measures of central value in,
  142-47
  measures of dispersion in,
  147-49
  uses of, 4,140-42

health, chapter 3
higher education, 75-76
hire purchase transactions, 113
home assistance, 92-93
hospital morbidity, 48-49
house prices, 67
Household Budget Inquiry
  as weights in Consumer Price
  Index, 119

consumers' expenditure in,
  111
distribution of income in,
  103-04
sampling procedure in, 191-
  92
housing, 10,12, chapter 4

ill health, 46-53
income distribution, 101-04,
  107
income statistics, 98-107
index, price, 115-22, 124
infant mortality rate, 22
infectious diseases, 49
inference, statistical, 171-83,
  189
injury benefit, 90-91
insurance, social, 81-82,87-92
internal migration, 30,31·32
Irish language (1961 census), 11
Irish Marketing Surveys, 134-
  35,193-95

Joint National Media Research
  Survey, 134-35,193
justice, 131-32

law and order, 131-32
life table death rate, 19-21

live register, 84-86
Lorenz curve
  construction of, 149-55
  in wealth distribution, 105-
  06

market research surveys, 192-93

maternal mortality rate, 23

mean, arithmetic, 142-44,145-47

mean expectation of life, 19-20

measures
of central value, 142-47
of dispersion, 147-49

media, the, 133-35, 193-95

median,144-47

Medico-Social Research Board, 48,49,50

mental illness, 49-50

migration, 28-32

morbidity, 46-53

mortality, 17-23,36-46,51

moving averages, 160-64

multi-stage sampling, 187-88

national income accounts, 99-101

null hypothesis, 181-82

occupation breakdown, 9-10

occupational
injuries, 90-91
insurance, 90-91
mortality rates, 41-45

old age pensions, 87-90

ophthalmic health, 52

parameters, population, 173

participation rates, 74-75

party affiliation, 131

passenger movements, external, 29

pensions, 87-90,92

pensioners' benefits, 89-90

personal expenditure, 108-112

personal income, 98,101-04

pilot survey, 171-72

population
definition, 170-71
parameters, 173

Population, Census of, 1-14,25, 28-31

price index, 115-22,124

primary eduction, 73

prisons, 132

proportional representation, 130

prosecutions, 132

questionnaires, 172-73

quota sample, 188-89

radio
analysis of output, 133-34
licences, 112

random sample, 173-88

religious denominations, 10

rents, 67

Report on public preference for a second television channel, 193-95

representative sample, 171

sample
multi-stage, 187-88
quota, 188-89

random, 173-88
simple random, 174-83
stratified random, 184-86
sample surveys, 6-7,131,
chapter 10
sampling frame, 183,186-88
seasonal variation
in time series analysis,
157-64
in unemployment, 86
secondary education, 73-74
significance tests, 180-82
simple random sample, 174-83
social assistance, 82-83,87-92
social insurance, 81-82,87-92
social security, chapter 6
standard deviation, 147-49,
176-78
standard error, 176-77
in stratified random sampling,
184-85
standard of living, chapter 7
Standardised Mortality Ratios
(SMR), 39-40,43-45
statistical inference, 171-83
189
statistical methods, chapter 9
stillbirth rate, 22
stratified random sample,
184-86
survey methods, chapter 10

telephone statistics, 112
television
analysis of output, 133-34
licences, 112
report of survey on second
channel, 193-95
tests of significance, 180-82

time series analysis, 5,7,155-
67
tourist expenditure abroad,
114
treatment benefit, 91-92

unemployment, 83-87

variable
continuous, 142
discrete, 142
variance
in simple random sampling,
176
in stratified random
sampling, 185
use of, 147-49
vital statistics, chapter 2
vocational education, 74

wage rates, 102
wealth distribution, 104-07
welfare allowances, 52
'wet time' insurance, 87
widows pensions, 92